# A Life Worth Living

Kenneth Kehl

*A Boy Tempered by Fire
Becomes a Man Filled
with Love*

# A Life Worth Living

XULON ELITE

Xulon Press Elite
2301 Lucien Way #415
Maitland, FL 32751
407.339.4217
www.xulonpress.com

© 2022 by Kenneth Kehl

All rights reserved solely by the author. The author guarantees all contents are original and do not infringe upon the legal rights of any other person or work. No part of this book may be reproduced in any form without the permission of the author.

Due to the changing nature of the Internet, if there are any web addresses, links, or URLs included in this manuscript, these may have been altered and may no longer be accessible. The views and opinions shared in this book belong solely to the author and do not necessarily reflect those of the publisher. The publisher therefore disclaims responsibility for the views or opinions expressed within the work.

Unless otherwise indicated, Scripture quotations taken from the New American Standard Bible (NASB). Copyright © 1960, 1962, 1963, 1968, 1971, 1972, 1973, 1975, 1977, 1995 by The Lockman Foundation. Used by permission. All rights reserved.

Paperback ISBN-13: 978-1-6628-4381-5
Ebook ISBN-13: 978-1-6628-4382-2

# TABLE OF CONTENTS

Acknowledgments . . . . . . . . . . . . . . . . . . . . . . . . . . . . . . . . . . vii
Foreword . . . . . . . . . . . . . . . . . . . . . . . . . . . . . . . . . . . . . . . . . . ix
Preface . . . . . . . . . . . . . . . . . . . . . . . . . . . . . . . . . . . . . . . . . . xiii
**Chapter 1**   *Introduction: Bobby's Journey* . . . . . . . . . . . . . . . . . . . . 1
**Chapter 2**   *Natural Man* . . . . . . . . . . . . . . . . . . . . . . . . . . . . . . . . 9
**Chapter 3**   *Puppy Love* . . . . . . . . . . . . . . . . . . . . . . . . . . . . . . . . . 18
**Chapter 4**   *Joining Up* . . . . . . . . . . . . . . . . . . . . . . . . . . . . . . . . . 30
**Chapter 5**   *Civilian Life* . . . . . . . . . . . . . . . . . . . . . . . . . . . . . . . . 39
**Chapter 6**   *A New Life* . . . . . . . . . . . . . . . . . . . . . . . . . . . . . . . . . 43
**Chapter 7**   *House Calls* . . . . . . . . . . . . . . . . . . . . . . . . . . . . . . . . . 49
**Chapter 8**   *The Move* . . . . . . . . . . . . . . . . . . . . . . . . . . . . . . . . . . 55
**Chapter 9**   *Disenchantment* . . . . . . . . . . . . . . . . . . . . . . . . . . . . . 62
**Chapter 10**   *The Pastor* . . . . . . . . . . . . . . . . . . . . . . . . . . . . . . . . . 67
**Chapter 11**   *Supernatural Experiences* . . . . . . . . . . . . . . . . . . . . . . 72
**Chapter 12**   *Preparation* . . . . . . . . . . . . . . . . . . . . . . . . . . . . . . . . 78
**Chapter 13**   *Learning the Basics* . . . . . . . . . . . . . . . . . . . . . . . . . . . 86
**Chapter 14**   *The Family* . . . . . . . . . . . . . . . . . . . . . . . . . . . . . . . . 93
**Chapter 15**   *Coming Home* . . . . . . . . . . . . . . . . . . . . . . . . . . . . . 101
**Chapter 16**   *Matchmaker and Life* . . . . . . . . . . . . . . . . . . . . . . . . 108

| | | |
|---|---|---|
| **Chapter 17** | *Do You Believe in Miracles?* | 115 |
| **Chapter 18** | *What Are the Rules of Prayer?* | 121 |
| **Chapter 19** | *A Time of Angels and Demons* | 129 |
| **Chapter 20** | *People Who Have Influenced My Life* | 136 |
| **Chapter 21** | *New Challenges* | 145 |
| **Chapter 22** | *If I Were President of the USA* | 151 |
| **Chapter 23** | *The Future* | 159 |
| **Chapter 24** | *Encounter* | 163 |
| **Chapter 25** | *Conclusion* | 166 |

# ACKNOWLEDGMENTS

I want to thank my loving and gracious heavenly Father for restoring me to the person God created me to be.

I want to praise my loving wife and three daughters for putting up with me during this transformation of my life and to tell them that the best is yet to come.

Many thanks to my daughter Kate and son-in-law Michael Gomes for editing my book; they did a professional job, and I'm proud of them for taking on such a big project.

My parents, who did all they knew how to do in raising a boy who had wondering feet and a trying disposition.

Friends are the building blocks one's life is built upon. Without friends, the building would not be foundationally sound. The cornerstone of my foundation is my friend Jesus Christ, who holds my whole building together.

To all my teachers who tried their best with the knowledge they had in dealing with a hyper and dyslexic boy. A special thanks to my teachers who encouraged me and figured out my capabilities. It's got to be hard to teach a boy who misses fifty to sixty days of school a year.

And to all my very dear grandchildren, who have been so kind to my wife and me. They are the delight of our lives.

# FOREWORD

If my dad were a song, he would have to be "Amazing Grace." The lyrics could have been written for him and many of us. I've included them in case some of you may not know the words. As you read it, meditate on the words; there is truth in it for you. For me, this song always brings tears to my eyes because it is true, not only for my dad, but for me and many others as well.

**Amazing Grace**

Amazing grace! How sweet the sound
That saved a wretch like me!
I once was lost, but now am found;
Was blind, but now I see.

'Twas grace that taught my heart to fear,
And grace my fears relieved;
How precious did that grace appear
The hour I first believed.

Through many dangers, toils, and snares,
I have already come;
'Tis grace hath brought me safe thus far,
And grace will lead me home.

The Lord has promised good to me,
His word my hope secures;
He will my shield and portion be,
As long as life endures.

Yea, when this flesh and heart shall fail,
And mortal life shall cease,
I shall possess, within the veil,
A life of joy and peace.

The world shall soon dissolve like snow,
The sun refuse to shine;
But God, who called me here below,
Shall be forever mine.

When we've been there ten thousand years,
Bright shining as the sun,
We've no less days to sing God's praise
Than when we'd first begun.

(Public domain)

You see, my dad came from humble beginnings, to say the least. He was raised in a poor family by an alcoholic mother and absent father. He was neglected in every way.

Many who have lived a life like this take it as an excuse for making poor choices, becoming bitter, turning into monsters, or to check out on life instead of turning to the Giver of life and asking for help. Even though my dad went down that road for a while, he was convicted when he had an encounter with the Lord Jesus Christ.

When he repented and allowed the Lord to take control of his life, he became a new creation. You notice that I didn't just say he accepted what Jesus did for him; that is only part of what we need to do to have a new life. We need to give up control of our lives to the One who created us and ultimately has control of our lives anyway. We only deceive ourselves and make a mess of everything when we think our lives are ours to control.

My dad experienced a miracle in his life when the Lord immediately delivered him of alcoholism, among other things. I think that this was God's mercy, not only for my dad but for my mom, sisters, and me as well.

I think the Lord must have said, "This one is so messed up that I need to have an abundance of grace, amazing grace, for him and deliver him of at least these things, or he and his family might not make it at all." Thank you, God.

Even though he was delivered of a lot right away, there was quite a bit of stuff my dad still needed to make conscious choices about every day to leave out of his life. It wasn't easy for him, and it wasn't easy for us who had to live with him. Don't get me wrong, I think my dad was a good dad, and he did the very best he knew how, but we all experience growing pains and, unfortunately, as a family, we all get to share in those growing pains. I thank God that my dad loved the Lord and us enough to continue making the hard choices every day to leave behind those things that were detrimental, not only to him but to us as well. I know it is only because of his deep love for and relationship with Jesus Christ that he did not give up.

When I read about my dad's life, there were so many things that I didn't know about him, and I am so glad that I didn't know that man. The man he was before he got saved is not the same man that I know now. The Bible says, "He who is forgiven much, loves much" (Luke 24:47).

The man I know now loves much. It still amazes me that God can take such a rough, beat-up, old piece of clay and make something beautiful out of it.

My dad taught me to love Jesus because without Him, life is plain ugly. He taught me how to love people because they belong to Jesus. He taught me that it's okay to play, even as an adult, because life is serious enough. He has taught me to have a good, positive attitude in life, no matter what is going on around me. He showed me how to love my family and that it's okay to fight with them sometimes; we are family after all, and we stick together, no matter what. He has always accepted me and those around him for who they are.

The older my dad gets, the better he gets, and as he has stated in his book, God's not done with him yet, but I think he's come a long, long, long way.

*Kate Gomes*

# PREFACE

When you reach the age of eighty you wonder how your life might have turned out had you not made the decisions you made. Then you start thinking of how you could communicate the good decisions you made to your children and grandchildren or, in some cases, great-grandchildren. Everyone wants to leave a legacy that will help others in their journey through life. You would think that being the president of the United States of America would be a great legacy to leave, but how many people even remember or care who the president was forty years ago. Some people on the street don't even know who the president is today. You may be one of many who don't really care about what people who don't know you remember about you, but you probably care what your family and friends think about you. So I'm writing this book for those I have known and who have known me in this life.

In writing this book about my life, I have remembered some important things about myself, such as how I treated people and how people treated me. Each stage of our lives brings its own challenges. With each challenge we face in life, people play an important part in helping us become who we are today. I have included some of those people in this book to honor them. We have lost the art of honoring those who have given us a part of themselves. My intentions were not to write about negative incidents in my life but about those incidents that made a change in my life in a positive way. If some of the people I know don't see themselves in this book, it's because I do not mention names of those living.

I do not think in writing this book that anyone will look back forty years from now and remember who I was, but it's nice to know that people can know me better by reading this book now.

A friend of mine asked me this question. "Why is it that you have remained so quiet all these years?" I replied, "If you are out front and outspoken, you make yourself a target."

In my younger years, I didn't want to be a target. Now that I am seventy, I can take being a target better than when I was younger and angry. Being eighty-three doesn't mean I don't have a temper; it just means that now, instead of killing you, I let you live.

As you read, my hope is that you consider the stages of life I have gone through just as you and many others go through while here on this earth. With each stage, we diminish physically but increase in knowledge and understanding. These two ingredients make up what we call wisdom. I encourage everyone to write out their life but not until they are at least seventy because it seems to come together after that.

**Bobby standing to the left of his mom**

# PREFACE

Sometimes you can create something out of a little of nothing. This is the way it was with Bobby, who was not much of anything; but because of a miracle, his life was transformed, he became a new creation, put back together and restored to his original design.

To set the stage, I must give you some information about what was broken and how it was restored. This is where Bobby comes into the equation; it is about his brokenness and restoration.

*Kenneth Kehl*

# *Chapter 1*
# INTRODUCTION: BOBBY'S JOURNEY

In a small town in the middle of the United States of America, people were trying to recover from the Great Depression. Most of the country had begun to recover except this town. It was hit hard by the financial devastation of the Depression. There were five major railroad companies who had their railheads in this town. A railhead is the railroad's place to build and repair trains. It was also the shipping hub for cattle being driven up from the Southwest. It was a place that had a lot of different people coming and going, and not the best kind of people.

This brought trail drivers, railroad men, gambling halls, and houses of prostitution that created an open-town culture (think Tijuana in 1920, only white) that remains to this day. Perhaps today it is more hidden than open as in the early days. At one time during World War II, there were over 500 houses of prostitution, sixty gambling halls, over one hundred saloons and four military bases within twenty miles of the city limits. On any given Friday night, there could be as many as five thousand, young energetic men looking for a good time.

Gangsters from Chicago, Saint Louis, Kansas City, Wichita, and Little Rock would look at this town as their playground because it was more open than their own towns. Thus, anything went—culture provided the growing atmosphere for Bobby's early years of training and development. Have you ever had a recurring nightmare and felt you lived every second of it? Picture Dante's Inferno and add pain, and then you know the culture Bobby lived in every day of his young life.

Let's say, starting at age five, you were exposed to perverted sex, prostitution, stealing, killings, gun battles, beatings, fights on the public streets, and you were left alone and unprotected. How would you have turned out? Would that culture change your thinking and actions towards people? Would seeing the police stand by and simply watch these actions give you any security at all?

Bobby was born in Tiny Town, USA, in a small house with three bedrooms just a little bigger than closets. Some people's closets today would be bigger than these bedrooms. There was no running water or indoor facilities. His mother was a farm girl who ran off and got married at the age of sixteen, and Bobby was the second child born into this family. He had an older sister and younger brother. His father was a farm hand and twenty years of age. Their weekly earnings were two dollars. The condition of the house was not much, and his mother did what she could to keep it clean.

Bobby's great grandfather was a businessman in the town and had been affiliated with Jesse James and the Dalton Gang when he homesteaded in New Mexico.

Bobby's grandfather was a gambler, womanizer, and alcoholic. He traded horses, cattle, mules, and goats. He was Bobby's first and only example of a father for his first ten years. He was the only one that spent time with Bobby. Bobby's father was MIA much of the time.

The best advice Bobby ever got from his grandfather was, "Bobby, you need to wash your hands after playing with a dog because they

## INTRODUCTION: BOBBY'S JOURNEY

are butt kissers, and you don't want someone else's butt on your hands when you eat."

Where Bobby lived, there were underground springs all over the place. People would build walls around one on their property and attach a bucket to get their water.

One day while Bobby's grandfather was drunk, he leaned over the wall of one of these springs to get a drink of water. He lost his balance and fell headfirst into the spring, catching his pant leg on a nail. With his head under the water and being very drunk, he couldn't get himself up out of the water, so he drowned.

Bobby's father had these men as his mentors but was so hurt by their actions that he lived in bitterness most of his life. His father kept score of everything his father did to hurt him and never let it go. He ended up treating Bobby the same way his father treated him, and thus passed on the bitterness to Bobby. At the age of five, Bobby's father was called away to fight in World War II. He left his wife along with their three children with very little income. When they were lucky, they had twenty dollars a month to live on. This was during the winter which, was very cold, and some of what little money they had went to buy coal for the pot-bellied stove, their only source of heating in the little house with no insulation.

Bobby's mother was still attractive and only twenty when Bobby's father went off to war. She worked in a shoe factory to help buy food and coal for the family. The hours were long and hard, and the pay was not enough to support the family. so Bobby's mother began running the bars at night and leaving Bobby (five years old), his older sister (six years old), and younger brother (twelve months old) at home with babysitters when she could find one, but mostly, she took them with her.

Running bars meant that you went from bar to bar drinking and looking for someone to bring home with you. There was Bobby, his brother, and his sister out all night and eating whatever they served in the bars. The hardest part of this was the men. His mother would allow them to fondle her in his presence. Then, in a drunken stupor, would try and justify it to him. This began his hatred for women and later took him into the brothels and gambling halls.

At the age of twelve, Bobby was stealing money off the bar room tables and drinking beer with the drunks. It was easy to see why he was an alcoholic by the time he was thirteen years old. His schooling was almost zero as he was dyslexic, and nobody paid enough attention to catch it, nor did they care. In his junior year in high school, he missed fifty-six days of schooling, and most of the time he was there, he was intoxicated. His friends were the sort you would find in the bars, gambling houses, brothels, pool halls, and on the street. The sad thing about it was that he was a good athlete but incorrigible and had no one to encourage him in sports.

Bobby would be gone from home for days without anyone knowing where he was. He would be several hundred miles from home, and no one checked up on him. He had been in so many close calls with death that the public records showed he was dead. Bobby had been in jail in four different states by the time he was eighteen years old and more than once in some of those states. He had become the culture he lived in.

How was Bobby broken beyond his original design? It was his circumstances that formed him into what he was. You notice I didn't say who he was because he had no idea who he was.

Let me paint a word picture of Bobby if you would have met him when he was eight, thirteen, eighteen, and twenty-five years old.

At eight years old, Bobby ran away with a couple of friends. They were gone overnight and were twenty miles from home when his friends got scared and decided they wanted to go home.

At thirteen years old, Bobby would have looked you straight in the eye and told you an out-and-out lie, and you would have believed him because he was that good at it. You would not have wanted your sister, mother, or aunt to meet him because he would have had one or all three of them in bed with him at once in a sex foursome. You say that couldn't happen, but you would not have known the spirit of lust and power of it that was in him. His own sister couldn't bring friends home because he would have them seduced before the night was over.

He dressed according to the dress of that time, and he was good-looking with a great, physical build. At thirteen, he had to travel over eighty miles to get a date with a girl not involved in the things he was involved in because no decent father that knew anything about him would allow their daughters to be alone with him.

Dancing was second nature to him as he spent most of his time learning dances from the Black jug houses where he lived and in Kansas City. He danced to tunes the average person had never heard and moved in such rhythm that it was enticing to girls. Elvis Presley could have learned some moves from Bobby. Several Black prostitutes even tried to get him to play a musical instrument because of his charisma.

At eighteen years of age, Bobby was forced to leave town because of his involvement in and with some crime figures he grew up with. He went to the post office to sign up for the military and found out he was dead, according to their records. The only branch of the military that would take him was the Marines.

Being streetwise gave Bobby good insight into other people, so he was able to make it through the training without being kicked out. He spent three years in the Marines, had seven office hours (that's when the commanding officer tried to give you an attitude adjustment before court-martialing you), and one preliminary court martial, which he was able to talk his way out of. It was odd that after each incident, he would make another stripe or promotion.

When Bobby finished serving, his NCO in charge said, "Bobby, if we wanted to start World War III, all we would have to do is send you there, and you would start it."

Bobby took that as a compliment and surged into civilian life. With the training he had received in the Marines, he was more dangerous than ever. One time, while in a bar, six paratroopers tried him on for size and soon learned they weren't big enough to handle him. Of course, later some guys from the Air Force tried the same thing, and nine of them decided to not try that again.

You see, Bobby now had fourteen years of anger and bitterness stored up. And he was just waiting to unload it on someone, anyone. It didn't matter who it was. He would not remember anything but the start and finish of the fight, but nothing in the middle.

At the age of twenty-five, Bobby was married and had a sweet little girl. He hadn't changed much now that he was married except that he learned to hide his actions and control his reactions.

After the military, Bobby went right back into the culture he grew up in and was back to his old games. He had met up with one of his old partners in crime and would be inducted into a crime syndicate and headquartered in Kansas City. With his background, he was a prime candidate for such a position.

Bobby started having blackouts and would lose an entire week, not being able to remember anything that happened during that time. Who knows what he had done because not even he knew. If only the partnership knew how dangerous Bobby was, they would have run from him.

This sets the stage for Bobby's journey back from hell on earth to become a human being for the first time in his entire life. The chapters to come are about a supernatural transformation in the heart of a man who had no love, compassion, tenderness, morals, or understanding of a decent life that so many people take for granted. It's a journey you won't want to miss.

You ask, "Well, how would you know so much about Bobby to judge him so harshly?"

Because I am Bobby, and this is my story.

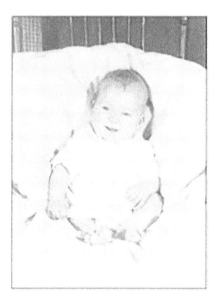

Bobby as an infant

Caption: Bobby with Big Sis Peggy

Bobby on the right with big sister and little brother

# Chapter 2
# NATURAL MAN

I gave a definition of good and evil in my first book, *A Cry into the Dark*. I think this would be a good place to remind ourselves of those differences because the world has switched the meaning of the two.

Evil is selfishly independent, engrossed in oneself, the center around which other things revolve, self-centered.

Evil will always give itself away when asked who benefits the most. One face of evil is that it appears it is for others' benefit. When the truth comes out, it is always evil that benefits. Nations have been built upon this single face of evil.

The lie goes something like this, "You are a nation of special people; therefore, you are superior to all other people and deserve to rule over those less qualified" or "We are a called-out people of God, and all others are less valued in God's sight. We have the approval of God to treat those not called-out as we are in any manner, we see fit, even if it means killing all of those who are not like us. The world would be a much better place with us running it instead of those God doesn't like."

Think of all the countries in the last sixty years who have believed the lie that they were more valuable than anyone else on the planet, therefore, making it their right to rule overall. Evil will always mass people around a common enemy. Evil will look for someone most people do not like and build a case against them. This will portray evil as the good guy. If it weren't for these people, we would have more. Therefore, these people are preventing us from having what is our right to have. We then must eliminate these people to get what's rightfully ours. Evil will present crises made of opinions instead of facts, then bring its own solution and convince people they saved the day.

I have been speaking in terms of nations, organizations, groups of people, and individuals. For what are nations made of but individuals? Individuals intimidate and make false statements as though they are true or could be true. They spread false rumors, state their own opinions, and keep repeating them until people start to believe they are facts. All of this is to gain some advantage.

Definitions for words like integrity, honesty, honor, truthfulness, mercy, compassion, and character have been replaced with statements like "the end justifies the means," "whatever it takes to get ahead," "they should have seen it coming since they didn't it's their own fault," "if you are so naïve, you shouldn't be in the position you're in," and "wise up this is the real world."

Since we are all self-centered in some way, does this mean we are all evil? The answer to this question has been answered throughout history! Yes, we are all evil and need a heart transplant.

If everyone is evil, then what is the hope of ever having peace on earth? Mankind needs an inward change that is so powerful it changes the very nature of man, which is evil. This is where every man and woman enters into the search for that inward change. There are so many roads to take, and everyone says they have chosen the right one, yet where is the change? What would a person look like who has made the change?

Mankind has so corrupted good that it looks like evil and evil, so it looks like good. Is religion, philosophy, government, spiritualization, the answer? Or has evil so permeated these institutions that it is a lost cause and mankind is doomed to destruction?

Like many people who were totally in the world and have now been transformed, we can't believe we did the things we did. It's like another person did those things, not us. For those of us who have had a powerful change inwardly, that is true. Through the blood of Jesus Christ, all things have become new; we are now a new creation. As I remember things out of my past for this book, it is a reminder of how much God has transformed me.

I was six years old when I pulled off my first robbery. I had found my father's silver .38 revolver in my folk's cedar chest. It was loaded and ready to be fired. My desire was for some candy, and I had no money. I remembered seeing in a comic book that if you pointed the pistol at the bank teller, they would give you money. I then realized that if I pointed the pistol at the man in the corner café, he would give me candy. So off to the store I went with the pistol. I walked into the store; there were several people in there.

I just walked up to the counter, raised the pistol, and said, "Stick-um-up."

I knew the man behind the counter because I played with his son.

He recognized me and said, "Bobby, you need something?"

I said, "Yes, I want some candy."

He said, "Well, you know if I give you candy, you will have to give me the pistol in trade."

The people in the restaurant had moved away from me with looks of panic on their faces. I thought it was a good trade, so I agreed, and we made the trade.

It wasn't long before my dad showed up at the house yelling at me about his pistol, but I had the candy and didn't have any use for the pistol anymore. My dad took the pistol to my grandfathers after that.

I didn't know the danger of my actions, and had I pulled the trigger, I might have killed someone because the pistol was fully loaded.

Would this have been an evil act by a six-year-old? The answer is yes because it was for selfish gain. Did I see it as evil at six years old? No, because there were no life experiences that told me my actions were selfish and dangerous to others. It is in our DNA to be self-centered and selfish. We do not have to be taught this; it is part of the fallen nature of mankind.

My brother was four years younger than me and was like any younger brother trying to be a part of his older brother's life. He always asked questions and bothered me all the time. We were staying at my grandfather's farm, and he was bugging me. I was told to watch after him by my grandmother.

We were in the barn yard lot and there was a young calf there. My brother kept asking me if he could ride the baby cow. Finally, I said, "If I let you ride the baby cow, would you leave me alone?" He said he would. So I put a rope on the baby cow and put my little brother on the calf. I thought if I tied him on, he wouldn't fall off and get hurt. I found some twine and tied him onto the calf by tying his feet together under the calf. As I led the calf around the barn yard, it decided it didn't like my brother on it and began to buck and run. I wasn't strong enough to hold it, and it got away from me. There was my little brother hanging onto the calf's neck with his feet tied together and sticking straight up on top of the calf while the rest of him was hanging underneath the calf.

My grandfather saw what was going on and came running and yelling at me. I thought he would beat me, so I took off into the woods. Fortunately, he caught the calf before it dragged my brother to death, and no one got hurt.

It was not my intention to hurt my brother. I just didn't want him bothering me anymore. I was trying to satisfy my own desire to be rid of him for the time. By this time, I had been taking care of him for over four years. It was always my responsibility to take care of my little brother, and I resented not being able to do what I wanted to do.

Why should a four-year-old have to take care of a baby brother just because the mother didn't want to? My resentment against my brother grew because I always had to take care of him. Give me a break! How could a four-year-old take care of a baby anyway, or an eight-year-old take care of a four-year-old?

When I was about six years old, someone took me to the movies or, it may have been I was dropped off at the movies. It was a Western, and the bad guys had been caught and were tried and hanged for their crimes.

In the very small three-room house we lived in, we had a wood-burning stove my mom cooked on in the kitchen. The stove had a large pipe running from the stove to the flue, and it had an L-shape to it. I remember my mother repeating her famous saying, "Bobby, watch your brother." Those were the worse words in my life and meant, "Bobby, you can't go outside and play with your friends."

I had a revelation and remembered the movie when they hanged the bad guys. I saw my brother as the bad guy. I held my own trial and found him guilty and sentenced him to be hanged.

I found some clothesline, put it over the stove pipe, made a noose in the one end, and tied the other end to the stove. I got the little stool that I stood on to reach things in the kitchen and put it under the rope. I then got, "Little Red," my brother, stood him on the stool, and put the rope around his neck. I knew you were supposed to say some words before hanging someone, so I bowed my head and said goodbye to Little Red.

Just as I was ready to kick the stool out from under Little Red's little feet, my mother walked in and started yelling. I knew when adults started yelling, I should run because a whipping soon followed the yelling. I ran out of the kitchen door and out to the outhouse, where I locked myself in.

My little brother's hair was red, and we called him Red instead of Carl Ray, which was his real name. Thank God that my mother came in when she did; it allowed Little Red to make it through another day on Planet Earth.

Red and I were dumped off at my grandparents' house in the country for a weekend. I was thinking of something to do when I came up with the bright idea to build a raft like Tom Sawyer and float it on one of my grandfather's ponds. I got a hatchet from my grandfather's tool shed, and off I went to build a raft.

I heard the voice of Little Red, "Wait for me. I want to help!"

Off we went to build a raft. I told Red he could not use the hatchet because he might hurt himself. Then a great idea came to me. What if the raft didn't float? Ah! Now, I had something for Red to do. He would be the captain for the raft's first voyage just to make sure it would float. Red was all excited that he would be the first to take the ship out and would be the captain.

It took us all day to build the raft. We finished as it was getting dusk. Red couldn't wait to get aboard and be the captain. I told him he needed to be tied onto the mast so he wouldn't fall off because he couldn't swim. He didn't care that it was the first time the boat would be in the water because I was letting him be the captain, and he was ready.

I tied him onto the raft's mast and shoved poor Red off into the deep. He was smiling from ear to ear and shouting commands. The logs I had used were green and heavy, and all it took was just the smallest bit of weight, Red; it started to sink. Red was halfway out from shore on a sinking ship and unable to swim. You might think he would be terrified, but he was so happy I let him be captain that he just kept grinning and shouting out commands. Now you wonder why I didn't swim out and save him, but I couldn't swim either. Here it was, getting dark, and Red was on the high seas on a sinking ship with no lifeboat.

Right about the time that Red started sinking, my grandfather came home, and my grandmother was happy to tell him that we were at the pond building a raft. He immediately took off to the pond, knowing his last experiences with us were not good.

I could hear him coming and yelling, so that was a signal for me to take off for the woods. He rescued Red, and I came up to the house when I thought it would be safer.

I heard my grandfather saying to my grandmother, "Nelly, what were you thinking? You know Bobby is trying to eliminate little Red." She said, "Homer, I don't think that's true. They are just being boys." Homer said, "Nelly, little Red is a boy, but Bobby is the devil."

This made me think that maybe I was the devil. If I were the devil, then I would have some power, and I needed to find out what that power was. Here I was at eight years old, deciding on finding out what power of the devil I possessed or maybe, it possessed me . . .

Thinking back over my short life, I thought of some of the situations I had been in and hadn't gotten hurt. Could this be the power I possessed? Maybe I was indestructible, or maybe I had power over others.

There was this time in the summer I was in a joint, which was a combination saloon, restaurant, and dance hall with gambling in the basement. Suddenly a gun fight broke out between several people. They were shooting at each other from behind the furniture. The place was full of people. Everyone was hiding. My cousin, who was sixteen years old at this time, pulled me under a table to protect me from the bullets flying around. I later remembered running for the door when some of the people were shot. As I stood outside listening to the police and highway patrol, I heard that three people had been shot. Two were doing the shooting, and one was just trying to get out of the way, but I didn't get hurt.

There was another time when my mom was with a carload of guys and gals who were drinking and partying. At the same time, they were traveling down the highway at high speed. I was shoved down onto the back floorboard of the car, where I couldn't see, but I knew it was dangerous because of other similar times.

I heard someone say, "Look out! You're on the wrong side of the road!" And a car or truck was coming.

These were guys from Saint Louis and were not good guys at all. With all the cussing and jumping around on each other, I was scared, so I told the devil if he would get me out of this, I would serve him. Just then, the driver passed out, and the car turned right off the road and missed the oncoming car or truck. It was pitch black, and I couldn't see anything. I remember sitting there waiting for someone who had gone for help to get us out of the ditch, and I dozed off to sleep.

When I woke up, we were back in our car and heading home. The sun was just coming up, and I had to get ready and walk to school. There were many times I would get home just as the sun was coming up and have to go to school that day.

I was with my mom in a honky-tonk, and a fight broke out as they did most of the time. I remember one guy was on the floor, and the other one was kicking him in the head. The man being kicked would cry out for help from God, but no help came. The man then stopped crying out, and the ambulance guy said he was dead. I know nothing happened to the other guy doing the kicking because I saw him in the bars later.

I realized that God didn't come to the man's rescue. I knew that if that guy couldn't count on God, then I knew I couldn't count on God either. I would stick with the devil's crowd because I had seen them help one of their own. It's amazing how a boy evaluates situations in his life.

Our babysitters would throw parties at our house when they were supposed to be watching us. These were the kind of parties where they would play all kinds of games. Most of the games had to do with sex. These parties were so much fun that we would invite our little friends over to watch the older kids having sex.

We picked up on it and started having our own little sex parties behind the couch or out back in our shed. This wasn't new to me because I would be with my mother at some of the same kind of parties. It was just the first time that I was able to participate with someone of my own age, six or seven.

Can you imagine the effect of this on such young children? This was a time I believe I had been given a spirit of lust that stayed with me until I was twenty-six years of age. Most people wouldn't believe this. I have lived through it. I can say without a doubt, darkness had come into my being and had control over me. I remember that when I would walk into a house of prostitution, I was like a magnet and would draw those of like spirits to myself without doing anything.

By the age of fifteen, I was an alcoholic, abuser of women, gambler, liar, cheat, con man, violent person at times, and a person full of darkness. What a life for a fifteen-year-old. The only thing I hadn't done was kill someone, but I had watched others being killed.

How on earth could someone like me be transformed into a human being with any good in me when I had only known darkness.

*Chapter 3*

# PUPPY LOVE

My definition of *good* is "benevolent, kindness that is above human nature and the surroundings it is found in."

We go through life remembering those who treated us badly, but how many times do we remember those who treated us kindly? My first years of being here on earth were filled with violence, hatred, distrust, and loneliness. I knew there had to be something more to life than what I had experienced so far. Trying to remember those good times was not hard because there were not many of them, but they were important. I can think of some people that, if only briefly, gave me another perspective on life. Some of these stories may not sound like they would be a positive experience, but even the hard ones helped me to learn that I had some value as a human being. So, I remember them as good experiences.

There was Bonnie Bodeen, who was the first good thing in my life. She was a beautiful blond, who was full of smiles and happiness. Her mother would run the bars with my mom, and we would spend countless hours in the car together. I remember singing country songs to her, and she would applaud my singing. She was in my first-grade classroom in school, and we played in band together. She had become my first friend and first love. It seemed everything she did was perfect, and I loved being around her.

World War II ended at the end of my first-grade year, and everyone's fathers were coming home. Bonnie's father returned home, and they moved to another state. This devastated me, and then we moved across town and to a new school for my second-grade year. I never forgot Bonnie until fifteen years later, when I met another blond named Sue, who became my wife. At this time, we have been married for forty-eight years. God bless her.

In the fourth grade, I had an English teacher I really liked. She would take time to teach me to read. I learned to read in her class. Can you imagine being in the fourth grade and not able to read?

Mrs. Wilson was a delight, and she encouraged me to be in our school plays. My favorite characters were Tom Sawyer and Daniel Boone.

I'm grateful to Mrs. Wilson for taking the time to work with a foul-mouthed kid who needed a positive direction in his life.

Our principle, on the other hand, was an unhappy woman. She was always looking for the opportunity to punish me. My language reflected the places of ill repute I was growing up in. About every other word out of my mouth was a slang word or a four-letter word that most people had not heard. I remembered all the jokes from these places and was asked many times to repeat them at school by the kids. I loved the attention and would tell these jokes to all the kids during recess. Then one or two of them would recite them to their parents. The parents would call Mrs. Cooie, our principle, and I would be marched into the principal's office to give an account of my stories.

After a while, I tired of Mrs. Cooie grabbing me by the chin and squeezing me till it really hurt. I took a healthy swing at her jaw and missed her. Well, that got me sent to the janitor's office, where he gave me several paddles. After a couple of trips to the janitor office, he asked me what jokes I had been telling the kids. I told him some, and he laughed so hard that he forgot to paddle me. After that it was, take a swing at Mrs. Cooie, go to the janitor's office, and tell jokes to him and several teachers.

Then Mrs. Cooie did the wrong thing; she called my mom. Now my mom was a hot-headed Dutch woman. She was even given the nickname "Dutch." The word Dutch in our town had a meaning to it. It was given to only one person in town who was hot-tempered, stubborn, loud, punched people they didn't like, drank too much, and would challenge the meanest and baddest person in town. That was my mom.

Mrs. Cooie called on Friday morning. My mom's weekend of partying started at 8:00 a.m. Friday morning and would last the weekend. Mom got the call at 11:00 a.m., which was only three hours into the weekend for Mom. She hated anything unpleasant that would ruin her weekend so quickly.

Our school was a three-story red brick building with wooden floors, where sound vibrated throughout the building in amplified vibrations. I was in my classroom when my mom showed up.

Her first words were, "Where is that low-life principal's office who doesn't know who in the hell she's talking to?"

Mom spent one hour in Mrs. Cooie's office, and when she left the school, everyone in the building had a lesson on the entire vocabulary of six drunken sailors in a cat house on a Saturday night. This was the first and only time my mom ever took up for me, and it was the first time I ever felt she loved me. For me, this was a positive experience.

I never heard any more from Mrs. Cooie, and she never called Mom again for the remaining three years I was in school

Bobby in the 8th grade

there. I heard that Ms. Cooie resigned from teaching the year after I left grade school. The janitors and teachers would ask me to come back and tell some more jokes to Bobby in elementary school, and I would go to the school basement and entertain them about once a month. I hated leaving grade school and Mrs. Wilson, my English teacher, but I had to go on to high school. For us, high school started in the eighth grade.

My first day in high school was traumatic, as I had no idea what it was like to be around teenagers. I didn't know that they thought the school was their school and people needed to bow down to them, especially if they were little scumbag eighth graders. Now who do you suppose I ran into the very first day? Yes, I literally ran into the biggest senior on the football team, and when I got off the ground, I let him have a string of descriptive adjectives he had not heard before. He then proceeded to beat on me and swing me around, letting me slam against the walls. Finally, a teacher came to my rescue. I couldn't believe it; someone came to rescue me. Typically, in my life, nobody cared enough about me to rescue me from anything.

Out of 20,000 people in my town, I had managed to alienate myself from most of the male population by this time. Of course, all the ladies liked me, and I liked them. I learned that high school would be a challenge and that I would have to change my strategies to make out it in one piece.

I learned that if you wanted to be somebody in high school, you had to play sports, dance well, and be tough and friendly at the same time. This was the beginning of my secret years. From now on, I would be one person at school and another person outside of school.

Up to this point in my life, I had not told anyone of my little journeys to Kansas City, Columbia, Nevada, Lake of the Ozarks, or Raytown, Missouri. I was a traveler and hitchhiked all over the state. I would be gone for days, and no one would check up on me.

I met up with a kid on the street who had a sister in Kansas City so we would hitchhike to Kansas City and hang out with the runaways on the street and in the penny arcade. This was the first time I met kids who were abandoned by their parents or parent and were left to fend for themselves on the street. This was the first time I realized that even as bad as I had it, there were kids that had it worse off than me.

There was one who seemed to be the leader of the rest, or the rest were just afraid of him. Let's just call him Joe. He had been in reform school for two years and had broken out. He told me about the things that went on in reform school, and I knew I didn't want to go there.

Kids were left at the mercy of the toughest kids, and they were abused in every way you could imagine. I think this boy, Joe, was about twelve years old. He never had a birthday party and didn't know how old he was. Joe was tall for his age with coal-black hair, olive skin, and a slim build. I think he had some American Indian heritage. Of course, everyone used the same vocabulary and acted tough. Joe could still smile but had a bad temper. Anger is a bad character trait in getting along with other people.

There were about nine or ten of us who hung out together at the arcade. I got to hear their stories over time and could tell they had not been as lucky as I had been. They had been damaged to such emotionally deep levels I doubt if they ever had a chance at a normal life. Some had been so physically abused that they were having problems keeping food down, going to the bathroom, seeing, hearing, and no one could sleep a full night because of the nightmares that haunted them in their sleep.

Joe invited me along with them one night for some "fun." I thought we were going swimming or to an amusement park. Instead, we went down to the river, which ran behind the City Hall buildings. There was a park there and the railroad tracks ran just short of the river. There were hobos sleeping by the railroad tracks and in the park. Joe said, "Now watch this" as he took out a pistol and went down by the railroad tracks; he shot a person there all wrapped up in bed clothing.

The rest of the kids ran over to him, tied the person up, dragged them over the railroad tracks, and rolled the person down into the river. They all stood there and bet on how long it would take the person to sink. Then they would celebrate the fact that it might have been one of their parents or some uncle or aunt. I realized then that this was their way of expressing their anger over their abandonment.

I asked Joe if the police would check up on the person they shot, and he said, "Why? They wouldn't check up on one of us if we were shot, at least they haven't in the past." Joe said, "You see, Bobby, we are no good to this city except to be used when they want to use us." At this time, Joe still had some light in his eyes.

Years later when I came out of the Marines and was living in Kansas City, I ran into Joe in a jazz lounge on Truce Street. He was standing at the bar with a couple of prostitutes. I walked up to him and said hello, but as I caught the look in his eyes, it was no longer Joe. He had become evil personified. I reminded him of who I was and asked about some of the other kids we hung out with. He told me that he was the only one left.

I never saw Joe after that, and another friend of mine who was connected in Kansas City told me that he hadn't seen or heard of Joe for a couple of years. Joe had grown up to be over six feet tall, had a slim build, and was very good-looking except that he had no light in his eyes. By looking into his eyes, it sent the hair up on my neck. He had crossed over the line where there was no return.

A guy I met a couple of times happened to be in town for a job he was doing for the city. His father, who was part of the syndicate, had a contract to resurface the city streets, and he drove the roller for the company. We met again while he was in town, hit it off right away, and began running bars together.

He was seventeen, I was sixteen, but I had been in bars so long that no one knew I was sixteen; they all thought I was at least twenty-one. He was from Kansas City, and we knew some of the same places and people. We ran bars together in my hometown all summer, and he went back to Kansas City for the winter.

He was in Kansas City during the Shriner's Convention, and some friends, Frank the Tank, Big Red (not my brother), Nance, and I were downtown joining in the fun. My friend from Kansas City said, "Let's go in the Mulebacks Hotel." We knew that a popular singer, Kate Smith, was singing there at the time. The Mulebacks Hotel was a nice, well-known hotel in downtown Kansas City, and we walked in like we owned the place and went into the Grand Ballroom, where Kate Smith was standing at the piano, singing.

I walked up to her and asked if I could sing with her. She asked what I would like to sing. I said the only song I knew that she had sung, "God Bless America." She said, "Great, we could do that," so she turned to the piano player and asked him to play the song. She then turned to me and asked me if I had any other request, and I said, "Just one more." She said, "What is it?" I said I would like to stand on the piano while singing the song. Of course, I was joking, but she said, "Do it."

There I was singing "God Bless America" with Kate Smith while standing on the piano in the Mulebacks Hotel, my big claim to fame, you might say. Kate Smith was a gracious person, and I have never forgotten her.

High school took on a new meaning to me as I became familiar with the social order. I played football and had a coach that was as tough as nails. He had lost three fingers on his left hand, so we all called him Stub.

He was a no-nonsense coach. His nose was pushed over to one side of his face and had mussels bulging out of his calves. If you didn't play hard, he would come up behind you and kick you in the rear-end to get your attention. Even though he was hard, I liked him because he was real, and you always knew where you stood with him. If you did well, he would tell you; if you did badly, he would tell you as well. You couldn't fool or con him because he came out of a street background.

His team took the State Conference every year for four years in a row. He was the only person who looked you right in the eye and told you straight up just what he saw in you. He told me one day that if I weren't such a party hound, I would make a great football player. Because I was a party hound, he couldn't recommend me to play at a couple of universities looking for defensive backs. I explained to him that he was right. I told him I wish I could be different, but I wasn't. He was one of those people who confirmed that I had value.

I was running with some guys who were in the Air Force. They were from New York, Detroit, and Chicago. I picked up on their accents, the way they dressed, and the way they danced. I lost my own accent, and after a while, you couldn't tell I was from Missouri. I had a language all my own, and I had adopted a whole new culture to go with it.

There was this girl, a cheerleader, who had been talking to me. We got to know each other well enough that she invited me to a dance at school. I had no idea how they dressed or acted at school dances, but I wanted to go with her.

I met her at the school because at this time, no mother in her right mind would allow her daughter to go out with me. This was a formal dance, and I showed up like it was Pacheco night in Kansas City. I had on a pink shirt with a black tie, a bright blue sports jacket that was long, pink pants, and blue

**Bobby as a senior in high school**

suede shoes. I had run with the Latin American gang in Kansas City called the Pachecos, and could they dance.

My date showed up in a beautiful gown. I took one look at her and decided this wasn't for me. I told her this was a mistake and that I needed to go. She convinced me that everything would be fine and that she liked the way I was dressed. She was a blond, and that carried a lot of weight with me, so I stayed.

The dance was boring, and the music was not hip enough for me.

Then the band played a song I was familiar with, so my date and I danced. No one had ever seen dancing like that before, and the kids wanted me to dance some more so they could learn it. It was a mixture between Latin, Black blues, rock n roll, and what we called White stiff dance. In the Lake of the Ozarks, you would have tap mixed in with square dancing, so I would throw a little of that in as well. I thought I might as well give them the entire package.

We had a great time, and no one said anything about the way I was dressed. I found out later that my date had passed the word along that if anyone did say anything about the way I was dressed that I had a shiv (switchblade) and would use it on them. She didn't know it, but I always carried a small .25-caliber pistol strapped to my leg as well.

My date's name was Susan. We became good friends, and I saw her at our thirty-five-year high school reunion and had a good

**High School Graduation**

laugh about the dance that night. She said she was scared to death that someone would say something about my dancing but thought that the way I dressed was great. I was thinking just the opposite. Girls—who needs them?

I had such a colorful group of people I related to at this time that I didn't consider I was different, no matter what group I was hanging out with. Back then, not one group rejected me, and I was always included.

Not until the people in the north decided we were all racists did we become racists. I really believe racists were used against this country to divide us, not to bring us together.

One of my early mentors was an old Black man named Nat Naugle. No one knew how old he was or anything about him. He was left over from the cattle driving days in the late 1800s. He found a trade in playing cards and rolling dice. He also ran liquor during the Prohibition and controlled what went on north of the tracks or, as some people called it, Black town. I learned a lot about human nature from him. Unfortunately, it was the dark side of human nature.

He would say "Bobby, always look into a person's eyes because you can see into their soul."

He always knew when he had a sucker gambler and would take them for everything they had, but if he had an upright person or had what he called light in their eyes, he was fair with them. In other words, he wouldn't cheat.

I had a cousin far removed we both knew. His name was Sheepshead (that was his real name because his head looked like a sheep's head). He lived in the Ozarks of Missouri. Once, my dad took me to Sheepshead's farm to buy some cattle he wanted to sell. Sheepshead was cursed or blessed with autism, whichever way you wanted to look at it. It allowed him to see things one hundred times faster than anyone else. He could deal out cards to however many would have been playing, And, then he could tell you exactly what each person had in their hand. He traveled all over the country playing cards for large amounts of money until people found out his gift, and then no one would play him.

Evidently, Nat Nougle had seen him at a big game in Kansas City, and this gave us a connection. I began doing some pimping for Nat Nougle at fifteen to earn some money. We had a good relationship until one of the gals insulted me, and I knocked her over the juke box. This put a wedge between us, and we parted ways. I had lost my mentor but that may have been a blessing.

I was spending more time south of the tracks and learning more about White people. I was missing about sixty days of classroom attendance my junior and senior years in high school, so I had to attend special classes for two weeks after graduation to get my diploma. After that, I took the entrance exam to Missouri University so I could attend. I was nervous about it but had a half-pint of Jack Daniels beforehand to calm me down. Out of ten or twelve who took the exam, only three of us passed it the first time.

I couldn't believe it! I was the last in my class in high school, and I passed the entrance exam to a major university the first time around. Of course, I was later asked to leave the university, not because of my grades, but for gambling, fighting, and causing a riot in one of the girl's dorms. I guess you'd call it a panty raid in college.

I returned to my hometown, picked up with an old friend, and started running the bars again. I was soon accused of being involved in something I wasn't, but the chief of police was not a friend of mine. He tried to use it to get me arrested. This used to happen to me in high school because I had a reputation; people believed that if anyone would have been involved in anything, I must be involved too. I decided to get out of town for a time, till things cooled off a bit. One of my friends had joined the Marines and was leaving in thirty days for the same reasons.

I went to the Marine recruiter to join. He ran a check on me and said that the information he got back on me said I was dead. I said,

"Well, here I am. Do I look dead to you?" That afternoon, I was on a train to Kansas City for my induction into the Marines. This was a change that would take me into discipline I never had before, but it was needed in my life.

# *Chapter 4*
# JOINING UP

When I arrived in Kansas City, I met a recruiter who was also from Kansas City. He took me to the hotel, where all the guys enlisting in the military were staying. I shared a room with about fifteen guys. I needed a shower, so I went into the bathroom. There was another door leading into another room, but it was locked from the other side, so I thought nothing of it. I was soaking up the suds when the other door opened, and in walked five gals. I could tell they were from the pony stable (that's a brothel), which was in the next room.

They were scantily dressed and full of questions. They wanted me to sleep in their room instead of the room I was in. There was no reason other than they knew who I was. I thought about a night with fifteen hot and sweaty guys or a night with many beautiful women. It took me two seconds to make that decision. So, I obliged and spent the night with the women.

The other guys were puzzled by this and wanted to join me until I told them whom these girls belonged to. None of them wanted anything to do with that. It was a sleepless night, and the next morning, I was awakened by a loud voice shouting in my ear. The person was yelling at me to wake up and get dressed as I would miss my ride to the induction center to finish my testing for the Marines.

As I was taking the exam in the induction place, I fell asleep. To keep me from failing the test, the sergeant took the test for me, and he flunked the test. After telling the officer what had happened, that I didn't take the test that he took the test for me, the officer passed me.

After the physical, I found myself on a TWA intercontinental flight to California.

**The Marine**

We hit a thunderstorm before we got to Dallas, Texas. The plane was a four-engine prop plane, and the storm threw it up and down so hard that no one could stand up. The recruiter sitting next to me had a hard time keeping his breakfast down as many of us did.

When we got to San Diego, California, we were herded onto a bus for the recruit depot. The bus ride was a time of instruction. I remembered having these kinds of instructions before lock-up in jail. I thought this would be more like a prison, only with a shorter sentence than I would face at home.

We were then taken off the bus and put in a large room with a couple of hundred recruits. Then a large Marine stood up front and declared we would not talk while in training unless asked to. I heard a couple talking in the back of the room, and the Marine up front went back, and I heard the familiar sound of a thud and then silence.

The Marine returned to the front and acted like nothing happened. The next fourteen weeks were the best and worst experiences in my life to that time. I wrote to a friend of mine, who encouraged me to go into the Marines and told him how wonderful it was in California and how great the Marines were. I didn't want him to back out of coming in since he suggested that I join. I looked for him each time we marched by the receiving station, and one day, there he was.

He had a lot of curly black hair the first day I saw him. The next day when I saw him, it was all gone, and his head was hanging down. He was a sad sight to see, but I got a chuckle out of it. I promised myself that whatever it took, I would get through it, and I did. I thought I was in good shape when I joined the Marines but soon realized it wasn't good enough. By the time I finished boot camp, I was in twice the physical condition and was mentally tougher, as if that were possible.

After hand-to-hand combat training, we were put in a large outside grass area, and about 200 of us were turned loose on each other to see who the last man standing would be. We didn't know it at the time, but this was the Marines' way of recruiting someone to be the general's bodyguard. About an hour later, there were only two of us left standing. I think I took a fall, as I didn't want to be anyone's bodyguard. That meant you take the hits for someone else, and I was way too selfish to want any part of that.

We were transported to Camp Pendleton for weapons training. At night, they took us through a live fire and explosion obstacle course. I couldn't see where I was and didn't realize that I had stepped on top of TNT charges just as they were about to go off. A second later, they exploded with me on top of them. I was thrown about 200 feet, and when I was thrown up, it was through a line of a .50-caliber machine gun fire. I wasn't hit but received some damage to my ears and the abdominal and groin area of my body. Everyone said at the training site that there was no way I should be alive, yet there I was, hurt but alive.

I was in the Naval Hospital on base for thirty days. I was taken into the operating room after I was given a spinal shot, so I couldn't feel anything from my neck down, nor could I move anything from my neck down. I was completely paralyzed from the neck down.

As I lay there buck naked without even a sheet over me, in walked a head nurse with her class of new young nurses for a practical lesson on surgery procedures, and she pointed out the place of the incision. The injury was to my groin area, so you know, nothing was hidden from God or young nurses, and all I could do was smile.

The surgeon asked me if I wanted to watch the surgery as they performed. I said yes. When I watched the surgeon cut open my stomach, I quickly changed my mind and didn't want to watch, so they screened me off.

All the guys in this ward were in for kidney surgery, circumcisions, or abdominal surgery. While we were in the hospital, all of the patients were allowed to go to a movie one night. The movie Bell, Book, and Candle with Kim Novak showed. She was the heartthrob of all young guys at that time. As I stated before, the kinds of operations we all had were with the lower portion of the abdomen area. After the movie, those with circumcisions were given spray cans of freeze to use in their place of stitches. All night, you could hear the spray cans used. The next morning, we heard that thirteen guys had to have their stitches replaced.

About a week after my surgery, I had a visitor. It was my old buddy who had encouraged me to join the Marines and another guy I knew from the same town. I still had one testicle tied down to my leg with a rubber band to hold it in place so it would heal properly. The guys thought it humorous to tell me jokes and watch me trying not to laugh as it would send a shooting pain through my body. They said it was beautiful out by the lake and wanted to know if they could roll my bed with me in it out to the lake. The nurse said it was fine. They rolled me out where I could see the lake. It was a tranquil site.

After our visit, they said they had to run to catch the bus, and they left in a hurry. Here I was out by the lake with no way to get back as I couldn't walk. I was out there for over an hour, yelling for someone to help me. Finally, a person happened to come out to see the lake and heard me. I guess this was payback for those wonderful letters I sent home to my buddy to make sure he didn't back out of going into the Marines. I would tell him how wonderful the Marines were and how much fun I had.

After Camp Pendleton, I was sent to San Diego for communications training. I spent four months there and was sent to North Carolina, where I spent the rest of my enlistment.

They called this the Cold War; it was anything but cold. We were constantly awakened in the middle of the night and put on helicopters to catch a ship in the Atlantic Ocean heading for the Middle East or to Cuba. We never knew where we would be from one week to another.

Once, we were off the coast of Cuba during a rainstorm in December. We were a recon unit going into Cuba to sight out Castro's hiding place on the West Side of the island in the mountains. We were given live ammunition and told we may be taking out Castro in his home. Then the orders would change, and we would be back aboard the ship. We would then be taken to the Naval Base in Cuba and stay there while our government decided what to do.

Similar things would happen in the Middle East, where we would show up on the Mediterranean beaches, running through sunbathing people on the beach. It was always a kick to see the expression on their faces when, out of nowhere, there were dozens of US Marines running through their lunches. These kinds of exercises would cause a lot of anxiety in the men because we never knew what each day or night would bring. At one time, we had 134 Marines AWOL from Camp Lejeune. That's absent without leave.

Sometimes you wanted to fight someone, and it didn't make any difference who it was. So we had lots of fights amongst ourselves (sometimes I think the Vietnam War gave soldiers someone to fight). I was given a security clearance so I could send and receive classified messages. Sometimes I would be gone for months and couldn't contact anyone outside our command. My mother wrote my commanding general a letter asking why her son couldn't call or write her. I could only imagine what she said. Whatever it was, it impressed the general. Shortly after his conversation with my mother, my commander called me into his office, told me to sit down, gave me a phone, and told me to call my mother. I did, and she was satisfied. I guess the general was as well. I guess he never wanted to receive another letter like Dutch could write, and he especially didn't want a phone call, or even worse, a visit from her.

While in the Marines, my character greatly changed. Before the Marines, I had no concept of honor, pride, commitment to others, purpose, discipline, value of life, and I certainly didn't know thirteen ways to kill someone in two seconds. Although these new traits sometimes contradicted each other, I took them on as part of my character just the same, at least while I was on base. Off base, it was still anything goes, well, almost anything.

My first experience with the supernatural happened while I was in the Marines. While walking down the sidewalk in Wilmington, NC, I came to a corner and stopped for an older black limo coming across the street, where I was about to cross. As it drove by in front of me, I noticed a Black chauffeur and a little old woman dressed in black in the back seat. She smiled as they slowly went by me.

After they passed by me, I continued across the street. It seemed strange to me, so I looked down the street they had turned. I was shocked to find that the street disappeared right into the bay, and I couldn't see them anywhere. They disappeared. I walked toward the bay to see if they could have turned down a driveway or into a yard, but there was no place for them to go except into the bay. This happened by an old, abandoned house that always had the front door handle and doorknocker polished; they were brass.

I went on to my friend's house and told him or her what I had seen. He or she confirmed that the chauffeur and the little old lady had been seen there before. No one had ever been seen polishing the front door knocker and handle on the old house, but it was always polished. The little old lady and her chauffeur were part of a love story. They knew there was no way their families would accept their relationship, so they drove off into the bay and drowned. Ever since then, on the anniversary of their death, they would show up in their car, and someone would see them drive into the bay. I happened to be there on one of the days it happened. It does make you wonder about whether there is something more in this life than we understand.

There were other instances while in the Marines that made me recognize there were questions that did not have a human answer.

North Carolina was a dry state, and you could only buy liquor at a state liquor store. The price was much higher than what we would pay on base, so a couple of buddies and I brought with us a couple of fifths of whiskey that we bought on base. We brought one to drink and one to sell to help pay for our weekend.

The three of us went to the beach and rented a room over the boardwalk for the night. Two of us wanted to go to a music concert while the other wanted to stay at the room. Upon returning to the hotel, I told the clerk that only one person was to stay in the room so we could get the lower price. I slipped my buddy by her, and when we found our room, it was locked from the inside. We couldn't wake the other guy up, so we went down on the boardwalk to find another way in.

I noticed the marquee was directly under one of our windows. I thought I could climb up and get into the room through the window. The boardwalk was light and full of people. I climbed up the ladder beside the marquee and onto the top of the marquee. I noticed there were boards lying on top of the marquee as a walkway, so I started toward the other side where our window was.

I was visible to everyone on the boardwalk, and a crowd began to congregate to see what I was doing. There were two iron supports attached to the building and the marquee to hold it up. I had stepped over onto one of these supports when my foot slipped off and caused one of the cables that furnished the electricity to the marquee to break. It began sparking and shooting lightning-like bolts between my legs. This, I thought, was not good. I looked at the window and could see that it and the screen were closed.

Someone below me said, "Jump, or you will be electrocuted!"

I jumped toward the window and found myself inside the room. I was so pumped by the experience that when I saw the other guy on the bed passed out with the empty fifth of whiskey beside him, I grabbed him and threw him across the room and up against the wall, which sobered him. I turned and saw that the window was still shut and the screen still closed, but none of it was damaged. I couldn't believe it.

The noise I created by throwing our guy across the room and against the wall caused the clerk to call the police. We grabbed everything we had and left the hotel through the back door. My other buddy on the boardwalk said he had never seen anyone leap through the air like that, and he wanted to know who the person was who opened the window. If our other buddy was passed out, and I was leaping, then where did the other guy come from? We will never know. Some things in life just happen.

My gunny sergeant called me into his office one day and told me that if the United States of America wanted to start World War III, they should pick me to start it. I had so many escapades that ranged from having unauthorized tours of the FBI Building in Washington DC, conning an FBI agent into paying our bar bill of one hundred dollars, partying with drug dealers in Brooklyn, NY, smoking pot in Greenwich Village, NY, to hob-knobbing with the Sicilian mob in

Cleveland, Ohio, and many more, not to mention challenging our general to give me an embassy duty in Spain. I had seven office hours and one preliminary court martial on my record, and after every other one, I made another rank. I was honorably discharged as a Sergeant E-4.

**Bobby when he was dating Sue**

# Chapter 5
# CIVILIAN LIFE

After being in the Marines for three years with three meals a day, a bed, for the most part, and discipline for the first time in my life, I felt a little uncertain about leaving. When I returned to my hometown, I was no longer known as Sergeant Kehl, just Bob Kehl, a civilian.

I spent the summer working odd jobs like putting up hay for farmers my uncle knew. There was this one farmer who insisted that my brother and I get his hay out of the field that day before it rained. We got it up into his barn as the rain started on the last wagonload. It wasn't even wet when we got it into the barn, but because he wasn't happy about it, he told my brother he wouldn't pay us because we didn't have all the hay in the barn before it rained.

When my brother told me this, I said, "Ok, we will take all the hay back into the field, and he can get someone else to put it up." I started loading the wagon back up when the farmer came running to the barn yelling for us to stop. He asked, "What are you doing?" "We're putting all this hay that you won't pay us for back out into the field. You can get someone else to come put it up for you," I responded. He said he would go and get his shotgun to stop us. I told him to go get his shotgun because then I would have cause to take his shotgun, put it where the sun didn't shine, and pull the trigger. He then decided to pay us.

A friend of the family told me about a job in Kansas City at the GMC Truck dealership. I went to apply and got the job in the accounting office. I spent several months cooking the books for the dealership. I was then asked to work in the sales office with a woman sales manager. She was single, about forty-seven years old, and was looking for an assistant. I soon learned what she wanted was a playmate. So I quit and took a part-time job in my hometown while going to college.

I saved up my money to eventually move to Scottsdale, Arizona, and work for my uncle in the plumbing business. For me, plans seemed to have their own mind. I was with some friends in a cocktail lounge one Saturday evening when I spotted a blond sitting with some people I knew. She was what I had been looking for ever since Bonnie Bodine moved away in the first grade. I went over and introduced myself to her and greeted my friends. When I returned to our table, I told one of my friends I would marry that blond. He told me it would never happen because as soon as she found out about me, she wouldn't have anything to do with me. One month later, we were engaged, and two months later, we were married. She did tell me that her friends warned her about me, but she thought they were exaggerating things about me. I assured her that they were.

We decided to get married on a Friday evening. We eloped and drove to Kansas City to pick up a couple I knew and then drove to Miami, Oklahoma, where you could get married in half a day. We stood in line at the justice of the peace behind a couple, and the woman had a little dog in her arms. I asked the guy which dog he was marrying. In my culture, that would have been funny, but he didn't seem to care for that comment. I don't know why; after all, it was a legitimate question. You would have to have known me then to have appreciated that comment. I had cleaned up my language a lot at this time. I could have said, "!@?>*&!# @." You get the drift.

My bride laughed all the way through the ceremony. I felt we were in a circus, and I was the clown. My friend's wife assured me that it was nerves, and she wasn't being disrespectful. This began a new season in my life and my bride's life. Nine months later, we had a beautiful daughter, I was working two jobs, and going to college fulltime.

I drove to college with three other guys. The college was thirty miles from my hometown, and this gave us some time to get to know each other. One of the guys was a Christian, and the rest of us were none affiliated. (Ok, that was putting it nicely; we weren't.) Every day, we would challenge the Christian regarding his belief in God. We tried the big bang theory, evolution, religion, and anything else we could think of, but he wouldn't change his belief. After a while, we realized we sounded more unbelievable than he, which intrigued me a little.

It was the end of the semester, and I had a job taking care of the college's copying machines, so I had to drive by myself. At this time, I went back to my lifestyle before the Marines. I had connected with my bar-running buddy from Kansas City, who was now in the syndicate. He had convinced me that my working two jobs and going to college was a waste of my talent, and the syndicate was looking for guys with my background and would pay well for it. I decided it would be better than killing myself for pennies and told him to set up a meeting for me.

I heavily drank again and went several days without remembering what had happened in those days. I was back to hustling guys at pool and using my winnings for booze. I played four Puerto Ricans in the back room of a dive-in town and took them for quite a bit of money, and I was the kind of guy who let you know you were losing just to keep you emotionally off your game. The more I harassed them, the angrier they got. I had been drinking all day and was not paying attention to their signals of anger until it blew up. They pulled knives on me, and I backed up into a booth with two broken beer bottles in each hand. Things were about to get ugly when my friend from the syndicate came in. He knew these guys because they had done some work for the syndicate. He convinced them to leave me alone as I was a candidate for the syndicate, and they would have to answer to them if they cut me up into pieces. They backed off, and I gave them back their money so they could save face. We became friends after that.

My life took a bad turn, and I went a week at a time without remembering what went on in my life. My wife was at her end of my lies and erratic behavior as was everyone in the family. I knew something was wrong, but it was such a part of me I didn't know how to stop or slow it down.

Finally, I blew up, knocked my wife across the patio at my folks' house, and took off in my car with only my undershorts. I drove one hundred miles an hour down a narrow road until I came to a one-lane bridge. I stopped on the bridge, got out of the car, and cursed God for ever letting me come into the world. I challenged God to show up, and we would have a go at it. Two weeks later, God showed up. My real life began at that point and has pointed to my relationship with the living God of all creation ever since.

Bobby in 6th grade in front of the house beside the railroad tracks.

# Chapter 6
# A NEW LIFE

Living on the other side of the tracks, picture yourself on a narrow blacktop road driving over one hundred miles an hour at 2:00 a.m. and aiming your car at the side of an even narrower bridge. Everything seems to be alright because it's just about over. The memories, pain, loneliness, and nightmares are about to disappear. It doesn't matter what's next because it couldn't be worse than the twenty-six years of hell on earth you've already lived through. For a moment, you are relieved, and your burden is lifted. It's like being born all over again with a fresh new start on life. The car seems like an instrument of mercy, and you feel you're floating in air—weightless and without any worry or fear because it's all about to end. Suddenly, you are shocked into reality, but it's too late to do anything about it. The next thing you know is that your car has come to a complete stop in the middle of the bridge, and you are outside of the car in your underwear, cursing at God for having awakened you in the middle of a good dream. What a downer when you realize you can't even do this right.

You curse God for having made you and just want to stop the inner pain of a life of misery. You hear yourself challenging God to make Himself real or get out of the way so you can end your life of hopelessness. You get back into the car and drive back home, where you knocked your wife across the patio and left your parents yelling at you.

It wasn't that I didn't love my parents and wife; I didn't know what love was. It's not fair to love someone when you know nothing about love. Of course, we were asked to leave my parents' house and ended at my wife's parents' house. They thought we had a disagreement and wanted to help.

We were there for a few days when I surfed the TV channels, looking for something with some action in it. Instead, I watched a show that reminded of California. It showed the Balboa Stadium, a stadium in San Diego, California, where I had seen the California story played out with people, horses, native Americans Mexicans. I thought this was the show. I sat my wife on the couch to watch it with me. I thought we were watching the beginning of the show. A man came on, and we thought it was a commercial, so we watched while the man spoke and made the most remarkable statement I had ever heard.

He said, "If you want a new life, you can have a new life, just by believing in Jesus Christ." I found out later that the man's name was Billy Graham.

I thought this was miraculous, and if anyone needed a new life I certainly did.

That night, I found out for the first time, that my wife knew about this guy named Jesus but had denounced Him years ago. I still had flashbacks and memory loss, but this statement kept replaying over and over in my mind.

That Sunday, my wife said that she and my daughter were going to this place called church. My maternal grandparents went to the same kind of place. I wasn't ready because I knew I wouldn't fit in. You see, I had met some of these holy rollers in the places I grew up, and they didn't act any different than me. In my limited knowledge, I figured if there was something to this church thing, then the people who went there should be different than me. My wife went anyway, and when she returned, I questioned her about how it was. She said I would like the teacher because he had been in the Korean War, had his left leg shot off, and he smoked. I thought it might be alright after all. So after three weeks of my wife going to church and telling me about it, I decided to go and check this guy out in case he was trying to put the make on my wife.

The next Sunday, all three of us showed up to church. I noticed a guy standing outside of the Sunday school classes; he was smoking a cigarette, and when he put it out and started walking toward the door, I saw he had a limp and figured he was the teacher. I decided I wouldn't say anything to him that week; I would just size him up. He wasn't one of the church people I had seen on my side of town, but I knew he had an angle.

We had to go into a room and sit in uncomfortable chairs. A big guy got up and said a few things about a party they were having on Halloween. I thought that was a good thing. At least they were party people, but I didn't know why I hadn't seen them before. How could these people live in a small town of 20,000, and I had not seen them before? Maybe they were the Kansas City church crowd who thought they could go to KC, where everyone else went, so they wouldn't be seen.

After the main guy taught, they broke up, and the women went in one classroom, and the guys in another room. I couldn't understand why they would do that, but I went along with it. The teacher had the same first name as I did, and when he talked, he sounded like he really believed what he was teaching. It was interesting to me to hear about this Paul person who went around telling folks about this Jesus guy. It intrigued me. After that, I thought it would be ok to keep going, so we went for several Sundays. Then, my wife wanted to go into the big room, where everyone went after Sunday school. I thought, well, Sunday school didn't hurt me, so maybe the big room would be alright.

The person they called preacher was loud and kept saying that some of these folks were going to hell if they didn't change their ways.

I found myself agreeing with him because I recognized some of them. They were not your nice people in the town.

I knew some of the prostitutes they hung out with at some of the gambling halls, and one of the men sitting in the church was married to a prostitute. He happened to be an attorney in town. I later blackmailed him into making me an apprentice in his law firm. The county prosecuting attorney had me introduce him to some lovely ladies of the night a few months before I saw him at church. He sat on the church board, but that was alright with me because I had nothing against a man having some fun in life.

I sat in the big room, and the music started. A group of people on the stage began to sing songs I had never heard before. They seemed to have a message in the words, but the music instrument the woman played sounded horrible—they called it an organ. I never heard an organ before and didn't care to again. The leader of the singers seemed to have a familiar look to him. Not the churchy look that I had seen before, but he represented something I didn't like. Later I found out that he left his wife and two children for another man, his lover. So this was quite a group but a group I could relate too. Maybe church wasn't such a bad place after all.

After the preacher went on about hell and damnation, people would go out the back of the big room and shake the preacher's hand. When my turn came, I thought I needed to say something to him about his preaching.

I looked him straight in the eye and said, "Maybe you would have a better response if you spoke more about God's love than his judgment."

You see, these people already knew they were going to hell. What they didn't know was God's love for them. The preacher didn't think much of my comment regarding his preaching, and we started off on the wrong foot. I'm sure he took it as criticism, but I meant it as an honest observation. For the next few weeks we attended church there, I continued to challenge the preacher.

The next Sunday we were there, the preacher, who hadn't taken my advice about his preaching, gave something called an "invitation" after he was finished preaching, and nobody responded. I wondered why anyone should want to join up when they had just been beaten up on for an hour.

Then came that song they sang over and over again, "Just as I Am." How else would someone come forward but just as he or she was? Then the greatest fear of my life happened. My wife lost her mind. She asked me to come with her to the invitation. I was stunned and immediately said, "Not in a million years." Then again, they played the song "Just as I Am."

My wife got up and walked forward like she had lost her mind. There I was, sitting in my seat, thinking about all the reasons why I shouldn't go forward. I even started to get up to leave, but it was like my butt was nailed to the seat. Suddenly, my butt came off the chair, and I found myself walking forward. I couldn't believe it. I got down there where several people were standing, and I took my place next to my wife. Suddenly, it felt like someone had me by the neck and shook me hard. I looked around to see who it was, but there wasn't anyone there.

Then I heard a voice saying, "Now you have really done it!"

Then something left me at that point. I didn't know what it was, but I knew something in me changed. After church, we went to my wife's folks' house, and her mom asked me what had happened to me. I thought, *How I can describe this except to just say it?*

I said, "Well, my heart feels like it has been taken out of me, and someone is tickling it with a feather. I think for the first time in my life, I have feelings for my daughter and wife."

No one knew quite what to do with that, especially me. How do you explain something supernatural to someone who has never had the same experience?

Over the next forty-five years, it became easier as I found others to talk to with similar experiences. The rest of this book is a life of experiences that have given me confidence in my relationship with the God of all creation who looked down one day and plucked me out of all the billions of people on earth.

You may ask, "Why you?" All I can figure out is that He did it "just because He loves me." He has done it for many people like me, and He will do it for **you.**

## Chapter 7
# HOUSE CALLS

We continued attending the Sunday school class at the church. Our Sunday school teacher called one day and asked me to go with him to see some guys that hadn't been showing up at Sunday school class. I thought this sounded a little like the calls I used to get from my partner in crime when someone wasn't doing what was expected of them in the syndicate. So, I had prepared myself for whatever might happen.

Look at it from the perspective of the guys we went to see. Here was this nice Sunday school teacher coming to see you, and he brought along a guy most everyone had heard of as a "no-nonsense" guy. We had a different language then to disguise our true intentions.

I remember once when a couple of guys from KC came knocking on our door at 2:00 a.m. to get me to back them up on a house call. Normally, you don't turn down these invitations, but I told them I had just been saved, and if someone questioned me about the house call, I would have to tell the truth because that was what people who knew Jesus did. They understood and left puzzled and shaking their heads but knowing they didn't want any of what I had.

I didn't know what Jesus did when He made house calls at night. Here were the teacher and me in a garage with three guys working on a car. I watched these guys and their every move in case the teacher and I had to "make an impression" on these guys. While I prepared for a fight, the teacher, out of the blue, told these guys to bow their heads and pray. I thought someone better keep their head up and eyes open in case there were others in the place, but things went smooth, and we were out of there. We made about three house calls like this that night, and I learned that it wasn't just about going to Sunday school and church but also about caring for people. The teacher and I did this every Thursday night until I left for California.

My wife and I drove down a familiar street in town when I spotted my old partner in crime with another guy. I pulled over and asked if we could give them a ride. They accepted and got in the back seat. We had driven about two blocks, and they asked to get out, so I pulled over and let them out. I noticed as they walked away, my old partner in crime kept looking back with a wrinkled expression asking, "Who are you?" It was then that I realized I didn't have a connection with him anymore, and we had known each other for thirteen years.

All our before-Jesus friends stopped coming around, and we found ourselves with all after-Jesus friends. You see, whatever it was that left me was the only connection I had with everyone I had known up to that point; once Jesus came into my life, all the other things left my life. Other things changed supernaturally as well. I stopped having those weeks when I couldn't remember anything. I wanted to remember what happened in my life now. After being an alcoholic for thirteen years, I lost the desire for alcohol and drugs. The one thing I had been haunted by was the ability to attract women. Now I had no interest in any woman except my wife. Some things I stopped because I decided to, such as smoking, lying, cheating, and hanging out with those who did.

Because of all the changes in my life, I found myself without a job. How could I keep doing the things I used to do after what happened to me? I looked for a real job, but the job situation was bad, and no matter what I tried, I couldn't get a job anywhere.

My brother-in-law told my wife about places in California where they lived that were looking for people to hire, but I didn't have any money to get us there. Then I remembered the teacher always praying about everything, so I thought I could do that. I knelt beside my bed that night and asked Jesus if I should go to California.

No one had prepared me for how I would get the answer. I remember hearing the teacher talking about how this guy in the Bible would get messages from a dream or an angel from God, but I thought that was then, and this was now. Sometime in the night, I awoke and sat up in bed, looking at a person at the foot of my bed. There was a time I would have been out of bed and attacking the person who was in my bedroom uninvited, but I seemed to be at peace with this. The person was about five-foot-nine in height and thin. He had black hair down to his shoulders and olive-colored skin. His eyes were dark brown, and his nose was sharp and long. He had a beard and was dressed in what looked like a heavy wool robe, something a shepherd would wear. I had seen pictures of a man like him in the Bible.

I could say nothing, but He spoke this to me, "Go and tell them that my coming is soon." Then I sat up until daybreak and thought that it was Jesus, and He told me to go to California. Years later, I saw a portrait of Jesus a monk had painted, and it looked like the person who stood at the foot of my bed.

That day, I was to meet my father-in-law, go to the bank with him, and help him do something; he didn't tell me what help he wanted. As we walked to the bank, he told me he would give me money to go to California. I was surprised because this was a man who didn't give anyone anything. I went home and told my wife we were going to California and to get packed. We put everything we had in our little Ford Ventura and headed to Orange, California. The next day after arriving in Orange, I went out and got a job. Here we were with our three-year-old daughter, my wife expecting our second child in three months, and I with a new job, and all because Jesus busted my pants loose from the seat in the big room at church, all within one year.

As a meat-cutting apprentice, people who didn't share my enthusiasm for Jesus challenged me.

During my break one day, my supervisor said to me in front of everyone there, "Hey Bob! What would you do if I hit you in the face? Would you turn the other cheek and let me hit it too?"

I had an immediate idea to slap him, but instead, I thought about it and said this, "You know, Ron, I don't know what I would do now, but only a year ago I would take this knife and run it into your stomach. Give it your best shot, and we will find out." Fortunately for both of us, he never tried it, but it made me think about what I would have done.

In the Marines, we were trained to visualize, anticipate, and react to the situation. About ten years ago, I had gone over to a person's house to confront him on how he had treated my wife. The guy was belligerent. I pictured myself flying across the room, landing on top of him, popping his eardrums, and then pulling his esophagus out of his throat. During the anticipation of this act, I realized the consequences of this action and stopped.

I came to realize how all the stuff in my past was still in my memory banks, and only the Holy Spirit of God's restraint could stop me. Then another truth came to me later that told me if I didn't walk in constant relationship with my God, I could still choose to go back to my old life. This put fear in me for the very first time in my new life because I never wanted to go back to hell on earth.

I think when the Bible talks about the fear of God, it refers to our fearing of going back to the world's ways. Folks, the soul has been redeemed, but the flesh is still the flesh.

One day, I was off from work and in the house alone. I told Jesus how good I had become, and if He saw anything in me that was not good to show me what it was, and I would change it. The next thing

I knew, I was on the floor weeping and crying out for Him to stop because there was still so much in me that was not good that it overwhelmed me. I remember walking around for days mourning over the list of things on it that I had not even considered as not being good. It also gave me mercy for others I had considered less good than me. This was my first lesson in religion versus the kingdom of God.

I worked as a lead man in a meat department and was critical of the manager and how he ran the operation. I, of course, let my opinion be known to everyone around me, including the manager. He was a nice guy and married with five children and another on the way. I would get into arguments with him, and believe me, you didn't want to argue with me because some of that old nature would raise its ugly head. I had intimidated this nice guy to the point that his job was in jeopardy.

I became very ill with influenza pneumonia, and while my wife was in another hospital giving birth to our third daughter, I was across town, hospitalized in a quarantined room. Everyone who came into my room had to wear these masks, robes, covers on their shoes, hats, and glasses. They looked concerned about me, and that concerned me. I was in there for about three days. One day, this person came in and talked to me as though he was genuinely concerned about my family and me. At first, I thought it was the hospital chaplain, but then he mentioned something about work, and I realized it was my manager.

No one else had come to see me except the hospital staff, but the one guy I had caused the most trouble came to see me, knowing he could have contracted this terrible disease, which had taken over one hundred lives in California. I felt small and knew he had a far better relationship with Jesus than I had ever hoped for.

This young man lost his manager job because of me, and I told God I would never do that to another person the rest of my life here on earth. I asked God to give this manager a job that was twice the income as the one he lost. A few months later, he came to see me, thanked me for showing him he was in the wrong job, and told me that he had a far better job now. This made me cry with tears of joy overwhelmed with the fact that our Jesus would be so kind to both of us.

You see, we are not each other's enemy, but we do share an enemy, and his name is the prince of this world. We are the children of the light and citizens of the kingdom of God. I realized that God the Father loved me so much that He forgave me for every wrong I had done, and He wanted me to forgive others with that same love. It is the kindness of God that draws us into repentance of all our wrongdoings.

**A Good Day with Good Friends**

## Chapter 8
# THE MOVE

Now that we were in California, we wanted to find a church to attend on Sundays. There was a church only three blocks from our house that was the same name as our church at home. So, my wife and I loaded up our daughter and went to church. The people seemed nice and friendly, and we had a Sunday school teacher we liked.

Our teacher in Kansas City had one leg missing, and this one had one arm missing. For a while, I thought if you had a limb missing, it made you a teacher. I had started giving money in that little envelope in class. I was happy to give back to God because He had given so much to me in my life. I thought, *How much is that worth?*

We didn't know how churches should work or not work, so we were just glad to be with some people we thought loved God as much as we did. Well, during a Halloween party for the youth at the church, I found out that some of these people were just like I used to be—a mess.

We befriended a young couple we had met—the wife was the preacher's daughter, and I found out later that several of the deacons were having sex with her. Then the choir director, who was a female, and the preacher's daughter, who we befriended, ran off with each other. Later, we learned that the preacher was having sex with his other daughters—we felt it was time to look for another church.

My wife had met a lady in the hospital while they were having their babies (our third daughter and her second son), and my wife thought this lady was in love with God because she and her husband were always talking about Jesus. They attended a house Bible study at the time, but it had grown too large for the house, so they moved it into the church they attended. This was a Quaker church, and we thought Quaker Oats was good, so maybe this church would be good as well.

We became friends with several young couples our age and enjoyed the church. Our home group teacher used to be a pop musician with a popular band, and after the study, he would play a song or two, which was uplifting. Several years later, we, along with several of these same families, started a movement with this man by the name of John Wimber. We were happy, and life was good. We bought a new house in the area, so we could be close to the people we had come to love.

One Sunday, a missionary came to the church and delivered a powerful message that touched me. She weighed no more than ninety pounds, and she had a real hammer in her hand, and while she preached, she would use that hammer to demonstrate crushing the serpent's head by hitting the pulpit, and everyone would jump. She sure knew how to drive a point home with that hammer.

Sometime later, one of the men in the church started a Sunday school class on the Person of the Holy Spirit of God. I hadn't heard of the Holy Spirit before that. The teacher's name was Paul, and I thought since his name was the same as the guy I so loved hearing about in Sunday school, it would be a great class to attend. We had this little book from an author I had never heard of, and I wasn't sure what to think, but as I read it, I thought the information was too good to be true.

One Sunday afternoon, I was reading about this Holy Spirit and decided to go into my bedroom and do what the book instructed us to do. I knelt down beside my bed and prayed that the Holy Spirit would come and baptize me in Him. I didn't feel any different, so I got up and went back into the living room. Just then, these nice Mormon boys came by to tell me about their god. I opened the door and blurted out, "Come on in, guys," and the three of them fell backward at the same time on my sidewalk. I started toward them to help them up, but they jumped up and ran off. They never came around again, so I could never ask them what had happened to them. I did see one of them the next week. He was on his bicycle, and when I yelled at him, he took off as fast as that bicycle could go. I look back on that as a strange thing.

Things in my life I thought would never change began changing. I was in the mountains looking out over the valley where I lived. I could see as far as the eye could see. I had a vision and could see people throughout the valley with their hands up, singing to God. It was like I had x-ray vision and could see into their hearts and knew their life story.

I shared this with my Bible study teacher, and he said it was of the devil and told me not to share it around the church because another guy, who had a similar thing happen to him and told people about it, had the elders of the church run him off. I didn't want to say things that were of the devil and get run off, but other things began to happen.

During the song time in church, I would get this bubbling up inside of me and wanted to burst out in praise to God for all the wonderful things He had done for my family and me. I shared that as well, and my teacher said that the other guy also did that before he was run off. I started to think there must be something wrong with me if the devil was giving me these wonderful expressions of God.

At work, people started calling me preacher. By this time, I was a manager, and it didn't bother me as I understood where they were coming from. I had this one young man who, every chance he got, would be back in my area, bugging me about who Jesus was. I finally asked him if he wanted me to introduce him to Jesus. He was so excited I would take him to meet this Jesus he had heard so much about. So I took him to my home Bible study with me and introduced him to my teacher. The teacher asked him what he wanted, and he said to be saved. He and my teacher prayed, and he got saved. I thought to myself, *Well, I can do that, and so I did.* This was in the late sixties when even the critics were getting saved.

One day, the young man at work came back and asked me if I would take him to the Army induction center in LA because he was going to the Vietnam War. I never saw him after that, but someday I hope to see him in heaven, and we can catch up on our lives. I hate wars that take the lives of our young men and women who are so brave to go off to war but for the wrong reasons so many times.

Over the years, I have learned that in this world, we will always be at war because there is good and evil. Yet I have learned another way of fighting these wars without killing the innocent.

The fight is against the principalities and powers in high places, and we can fight these wars with weapons not of this world. We think of wars between countries or groups of people, but I say that everyone is fighting their own personal war every day.

At this time of my life, I was working fifty to sixty hours a week with a wife and three girls at home. On top of this, I was teaching three home Bible studies a week and trying to shove in some social time. What I was really doing was physically and spiritually killing myself. I was trying to pay God back for all the good things He had done for me. Of course, no one I knew would tell me to stop because it was helping them and the church, and those are good things.

Sometimes at work at about 1:00 p.m., I could literally not recall my name. I thought it was the stressful industry I was in and needed to get into another field of work. I would go home at night and sit and stare at the ceiling, thinking at any minute, I would lose complete control of my mind. I finally went to the doctor, and he gave me a glucose test and found out I had hypoglycemia, also known as low blood sugar. He said I was on the verge of going into a coma if I didn't get help soon. They told me to get a lot of rest, put me on a diet, and after two months, I finally began feeling better.

I felt the work had taken its toll on me, and I needed a change, so I went back to college to become a preacher. I traveled around the Quaker churches, filling in for other preachers as needed, and went full-time to college. I was asked by the Friend's Board to take an assistant's pastor position in a small Quaker church on a one-year contract. I was pleased and thought this would be the answer to my stressful job. So, I quit my meat-cutting job and became a pastor. The senior pastor was a man who had all but given up on this church and would take long naps on his desk every afternoon. I decided if I would take money for this job, I would at least earn it.

The first thing I did was talk to those who were at the church and who had left the church to see how I could help. Some told me they didn't want me there; others had been hurt by the actions of others in the church and didn't want anything to do with church again, and one person threatened me with a steel bar if I ever came close to him again. I guess these people thought I was like other pastors they had dealt with in the past. They didn't know my past and my resolve to get things done with or without them.

The youth groups were nonexistent, so I gathered young people in the immediate area. Our high school group grew from four to thirty-five in six months; our junior high group grew from one to over 120 every week. The adult attendants grew from fifty to 195 every Sunday.

I was given the job of preaching one Sunday morning and didn't know what to say except how grateful I was for the loving kindness of God toward people. There happened to be a professor of English and literature there that morning, and I noticed he was irritated at what I was saying or maybe at the way I was saying it.

I had decided as a point, I would give an example of this hamster my girls had. It had gotten out of its cage and was hiding somewhere in our house. One night, in the middle of the night, my wife woke me to inform me that something was in our bedroom curtains that was right next to her head. She was standing up on our bed and yelling for me to get it. I shut our bedroom door so it couldn't get out and discovered it was our missing hamster. While my wife shouted instructions from on top of our bed, I finally captured it. The analogy was that while the hamster was in his house, he was still lost.

I closed with an invitation for those who wanted to know God on a more personal way to come forward for prayer. This professor jumped out of his seat, came forward, and knelt in front of the church. We prayed for him, and he received Jesus as his Lord and Savior. This was a man of Jewish heritage, and he was well educated. I later asked him why he came forward, and he gave me a great answer. He said, "I was sitting there thinking, I'm like the hamster in my Gods house But Lost.

I began visiting people in the ghetto close by and loving many people into the kingdom of God. I remember this one lady whose junior high boy had started coming to our church, and she asked me to come by so she could meet me. One day, Jimmy and I went by his house, and I met his mother. As soon as I met her, I could see right into her heart.

I could see everything about her life in detail. This so impressed her that she started coming to church with her son and became a believer. This whole thing was puzzling to me. I asked some people about it, and they assured me it would pass. Well, it didn't pass; it got stronger.

I got a call one evening from a woman who attended our church. The woman told me that she and her three daughters were locked in the bathroom with her son outside the door wanting to kill her daughters with a butcher knife. She called the police too, and they came and arrested the young man.

She asked me to bring some people from the church and pray for them. I rounded up several people, and we went over to the apartment.

As we walked up to the apartment, I noticed a black Lab on the lawn out front. We were greeted by the mother and the three sisters, who were shaken up.

She told us that it was so strange because nothing like this had ever happened before. She said that her son, for no apparent reason, started cursing and threatening the girls. Then as he went into the kitchen to get a butcher knife, the woman took her daughters and locked themselves in the bathroom. She said that when the police got there, her son was trying to kick in the door.

We decided before we got there that we would pray in each room and put oil over the windows and doorways to each room. As we walked into the son's room, it was much darker than the other rooms, even though the light was on. As we prayed in this room, the dog outside began howling, and the room suddenly got brighter. It even became brighter than the other rooms. Everyone got a little freaked out. We were there for about forty-five minutes praying, then we said our goodbyes and left.

We got about two blocks down the road when we saw a black Lab in the road. It was the same one we had seen in front of the woman's apartment. Somebody said it ran out in front of a car, and the driver hit and killed the dog. I decided then that there was a great deal more about being a believer than I had realized. Some years later, I had the opportunity to pray for the young man, and he has been of a right mind ever since. What a miracle going from a killer to a saint in one prayer. In that moment, as in so many moments, I was so grateful that when I pray, I know I am backed up by the living God of the entire universe.

This started me on the journey of learning more about the gospel of the kingdom of God Jesus told His disciples.

## Chapter 9
# DISENCHANTMENT

I became disenchanted with the organized church. I attended our yearly leadership meeting of Friend's Churches at one of our larger churches. This was my first time at such a meeting. There was a lot of discussion, but I noticed that not much of anything got done. It was all theory and no real action. The leadership discussed how they should send a delegation to another church and debate the meaning of the existence of Jesus Christ. I got so irritated at the foolishness of this wasted time and lack of understanding of the purpose of the church. I wondered why we would want to argue among ourselves over what we should believe. I thought, what a waste of energy and time. Then it was opened to discussion for anyone who wanted to interject some thoughts into the subject.

I stood up and said, "Has anyone listened to the words that have been spoken here today? I have, and they are without wisdom. We have millions of people all around us who are lost, they don't know God, and we want to argue over whether we agree with each other on an issue that we all know but are not willing to share that knowledge with those who need it the most."

One of the elders stood up and verbally put me down as one who was new in the ministry and didn't know what I was talking about. I then said, "If Mr. George Fox—who was the founder of the Friend's Movement in 1650 in Northern England—were here, he would vomit over your statements. And since he is not here, I will go outside and throw up on his behalf."

I resigned that day from the Friend's Meetings. I was later offered a job as pastor of the oldest Friend's Church in Southern California but refused to take it. I stopped attending church then and stayed at home on Sundays.

A friend of mine called me and told me about another person we knew who delivered a statement to the church we had attended. It caused such an uproar that the elders decided not to let them come back to the church. I called the person who read this letter to the church and asked him for a copy. He dropped a copy by to me, and I sat in my chair and read it the next Sunday morning. As I read it, I began to see how I had been judgmental and angry toward the church and God. So I sat there, wept, and repented over my sin toward my loving Savior Jesus. I called a friend of mine and asked him and his wife to come over that evening and talk about the letter. They came over, and we discussed what we had become; none of us liked it.

Over the next week, we decided to start a home group, where only Jesus would be talked about, and no one could discuss anything about any church or other person. My friend found out that we could use the town's women's clubhouse to meet, so we set it up for the first Sunday evening of the next month. Before we could meet there, the place caught fire. A couple of days later, my friend called me and said that another friend wanted us to meet at his house, which was almost across the street from the church we attended. After Sunday evening church, we would all go over to our friend's house; there were only nine people the first meeting. We laid out what we would do and who would do what for the next meeting, then we prayed and left. The next Sunday evening, there was double the amount of people there. We started off with our guideline of what we would do. The first thing we would explain were the rules about what we could say and what we didn't want said. They asked me to read Scripture to give the meeting a focus point.

I read the Scripture in John 11:40–42 and said, "We are to be a people who sit at the feet of Jesus, and He is our only source of life. What we had done is what Martha had done. What we needed to do is become like Mary."

So our focus then was on Jesus, and His words became life to us all. People started having dreams and visions about what Jesus wanted us to become, all of which you could find in the Bible, but all we looked at was the work to be done and forgot the intimate relationship God the Father wanted with us, His children. We would then break up into small groups and pray for each other. One rule in praying for each other is that you could only ask for prayer for yourself, not for Aunt so and so, only for yourself.

In four months, this group grew to over a hundred, and we had people in every room in the house, even the bathrooms. It got so large, and the neighbors complained to the church about all the cars parked on the street when the church parking lot was practically empty. This caused the church to go into action to try to get us to meet in the church instead of the house down the street, but we could not make them understand that it was because of the church that people were meeting in the house. People didn't want religion; they wanted an intimate relationship with God, their heavenly Father.

We now had over 150 people meeting in the house, and it was evident that we needed to get a larger facility. We rented the Masonic Lodge in town and began Sunday morning and evening meetings. I remember the first miracle was a young man that had two slipped discs in his back. We prayed for him in one of the small prayer groups in the evening, and he was immediately healed. We then outgrew the lodge and moved into an elementary school. We moved five times in five years. We had people coming and saying they had been looking for us for five years and finally caught up with us.

There were many people healed through the people attending the church, but the leadership did not see any of the healings come through them. This turned the focus into healings, signs, and wonders instead of just on Jesus. Up to this point, the Spirit of God gained favor with all people from all churches.

We had to become what we didn't want to be in the first place, workers for God instead of intimate children of the kingdom of God. We had to begin teaching others how to pray for the sick instead of just loving and caring for them. We taught people that whatever we did, it had to be out of Jesus's compassion for His people. It was the beginning of the end of a very beautiful relationship with our heavenly Father. Oh, there were some healings, signs, and wonders, but the love relationship diminished. So often, marriage is over before the separation takes place, but the atmosphere certainly changes, and everyone feels it, but because of the work, they continue.

You can teach theology, practices, and religion, but a loving relationship with the living God only comes out of a heart that yearns for it and will do anything to get it.

Movements begin because of the deep need in people for intimacy with God, not out of works for God but out of a need for a personal relationship with God Himself.

I sat and wept over the loss of our lover Jesus and beckoned Him to return, but the hearts of the people needed to turn back to Him first. Not everyone in the leadership was there when the real love affair with God started. They didn't know how to turn the hearts of the people back to God. To just sit at the feet of Jesus and learn of His great love for all people, and then, because of this love affair, He brings healing to the brokenhearted, sight to the blind, heals the lame, casts out the demons of the past, and the baptism of the Holy Spirit who will direct the purposes of His Church.

Rules and practices instead of the Holy Spirit's involvement bring death to intimate relationships with God, our heavenly Father. This is why the church needs revival every day. People need to be reminded of who they are in light of who Jesus is that we are children of the kingdom of God and not children of this world. Who oversees the church? The Holy Spirit does. Who loves people more than his own life? Jesus does. We are a royal priesthood, the bride of Christ; we are adopted into the house of our heavenly Father. We are eternal beings designed to follow our lover Jesus, our Father God, and the Holy Spirit. If you believe you are what the Bible says you are, then we need to be humbled by the fact that we didn't earn it, but we need to believe and receive it by knowing God and His loving kindness toward us.

God started a movement out of that little group of nine people who met, knowing their need for an intimate relationship with God. I realize that movements can become poor lovers, but people can become eternal lovers of God. We need to keep our eyes on Jesus and who He is and love each other as much as He loves us. We need to forgive each other as quickly as Jesus forgives us, and then forget it as He has.

I had a dream about more churches starting in the area where we started, and not only there but in England as well. When I shared the dream with others, it went over like a lead balloon. No one even thought about going to England or starting other churches when we had just started this one. Our little church had so grown with God's favor that we were fast in drawing the church community's attention. We were now meeting in a 100,000-square-foot warehouse and seating about 2500 people each Sunday morning and about 2000 people Sunday night.

I'm going to describe to you the acts of God that I was a part of and witnessed over the next twenty years. I have written about a few of these in two other books but not in as much detail as here in the following chapters. This is only to show you how merciful and kind our heavenly Father is.

## Chapter 10
# THE PASTOR

The friend I first called to talk to about the letter read in our Quaker church came to me and asked me to start a church with him. He said that everyone was in agreement with him doing this. I was making a change where I worked, so I told him I would give him two years.

While I pastored in the church that had started in Yorba Linda, I received a phone call from a psychologist who had a patient who had just torn her office door off its hinges and was using it to poke holes in the walls. She heard that we prayed for people like this and asked if we would pray for her patient. I said, "Sure," and we set up an appointment for the lady to come into our office.

When she showed up, I couldn't believe her appearance. She was about five-foot-one and all of ninety pounds. My pastor friend and I took her into my office and asked her to tell us her story. She said that she was lonely and had no friends except the two who lived inside of her. At times, she could control one of them by smoking, but the other one would throw her around her room and threaten to kill her if she didn't do whatever it demanded of her.

We didn't want to know what it demanded of her. We told her that she could be set free from these two "friends" if she was willing to let them go. We told her that they meant to destroy her, and if she didn't let them go, they would never leave her. At this point, we had not tried to cast them out. One of them threw slime out of her left eye and onto the backside of her glasses. I commanded the spirit to keep quiet while we were talking to her. It tried to talk, but I commanded it to shut up or come out. It backed off and kept quiet.

She wiped her glasses off, and we asked her if she had ever heard of Jesus Christ. She said she had not, so we explained to her who He is and why He came to earth and died for all of mankind's sins. We asked her if she wanted to ask Jesus into her life and forgive her of all her sins. She said that one of the spirits told her if she did this, they could no longer be her friends, and she would not have any friends. We told her that this was a lie, and Jesus would be a much better friend than these two spirits had been to her.

We told her that all she would have to do was say she wanted Jesus more than these two so-called "friends."

She said, "Can I keep these two spirits and ask Jesus into my life?"

We said no because if Jesus came into her life, then the spirits would have to leave because they were of darkness, and Jesus was of the light. She asked what would happen if we cast the two spirits out without her asking Jesus into her life. I told her they would have to leave if we commanded them because Jesus had given us His authority to cast them out, but without Jesus in her life, they would get more spirits, come back, and she would be worse off than she was before. She decided that she couldn't lose the two spirit friends and take a chance of not getting any more friends with Jesus in her life.

A couple of months later we heard that this little gal had joined the military. I don't know what happened to her after that, but I'm sure she would have made a good soldier in combat.

Two friends of mine told me about a young man they were praying for in a room with only the chairs they were sitting on. This young man was about six-foot-two and weighed over 400 pounds at the time.

They were caught by surprise when the young man suddenly fell out of his chair and began slithering around the room like a snake. He then ripped off the wall board with his teeth. This is when they jumped up on their chairs and began commanding the spirit to come out of this young man. The young man rose like a cobra and hissed at them. They kept commanding the spirit to come out of the young man until it came out with such a stench it stunk up the entire office. The young man was set free and returned to his right mind. You couldn't have seen two happier guys than those two in the room where the spirit was cast out, and you couldn't have seen a happier young man who was set free from all the anger he had against his father who was a chief of police in a town in California.

This young man was a worship leader in my home group after that. He later moved into a ghetto with another young guy to reach out to the gangs in the area. The house they lived in was constantly riddled with bullets, but they stayed until enough gang members believed in Jesus and could carry on the work there. This young man got married after that, began raising a family, and we lost touch.

There were about a dozen young gals and guys who decided they needed to go to Hollywood and feed the runaways on the street. I got together with them each week, and we made sandwiches together. They would go to Hollywood at midnight and hand them out to the girls and boys who were prostituting themselves on the streets of Hollywood.

My daughter was a part of this group. She would often bring a runaway home with her. On any given morning after their trips to Hollywood, we wouldn't know who would be at our home for breakfast. These were damaged kids, some as young as eleven years old.

Sometimes one of the kids they fed was killed, and it would devastate the group. It was like losing a dear friend.

At this time, there were so many young kids running away from terrible home situations that the pimps were having a field day. They were using them like slaves. People would pay for the right to abuse them in any way they wanted. Any city that allows this should not be allowed to be a city or any country that allows this will not remain a country very long.

I was called one day to go over to one of our family's houses because the wife was in such bad shape, they feared she was dying. She had been fighting cancer in her blood for several years, and it became so bad that she was slipping away from this life. I had been there several times to pray for the wife and the family. This time when I walked in, she was propped up in a chair in the beginnings of a coma. I had seen the look before and knew unless Jesus showed up with healing, she was gone. I almost collapsed myself because the whole room was full of death, and it sucked the energy out of everything and everyone.

I put my hands on her head, and the only thing I could think of to pray was, "Jesus, give this lady Your blood in exchange for her blood." I don't know how to explain what happened next. It was like I could feel her blood leave her, and new blood came into her body. After about ten minutes, she straightened up and asked for a drink of water. Several months later, on Easter, she gave the testimony of her healing. Sometime after that, her husband was transferred for work, and they moved away.

A few days later, a man called the church office to ask us to pray. His wife was in the hospital to have a tumor removed from her head. She was a hairdresser, and many people knew her, so a lot of people were praying for her. I was asked to provide food for the family as the husband was out of work, and she couldn't work either. They still had teenagers living at home, so it was a desperate situation. I remember the first time I saw her in her house as I delivered food.

The Lord told me that this was not unto death and to continue praying for her and the family. I laid hands on her and prayed for her every time I brought food. She started to recover, and fifteen years later, she is still doing well and so is her family.

There have been times we have had to encourage and pray for this family as they went through some bad and good times. As a church, we have had to fight our way through this with them for several years.

One of the lessons I have learned over time is that church is not just a place of learning but a place where you put into action the things you learn. We need to put into practice the things we learn, not only in the church, but we also need to take them into our everyday lives, no matter what we are doing.

A young couple came to us one evening at church and told us that their newborn child had been put into a separate room at the hospital to die. The doctors could not do anything to save this child. I got five other couples together to pray for them at our house after church. As we prayed, one of the young men began sobbing and then wailing calling out for God's mercy for the child and the young parents.

You just knew God showed up because everyone could feel His presence. Then the Lord told me that if we would go to the hospital every day for seven days and pray for the child, He would raise the child up. Without ever telling anyone when to go to the hospital, every day, someone would go by and pray for the child. On the eighth day, the child recovered and is a healthy teenager today.

I have given you a few things to think about, and my editor told me not to make the chapters too long, so I will end this one here and continue in the next chapter some events others have encountered in the Spirit.

I've had some experiences that were out of this world, or should I say, I couldn't tell if they were out of this world or not. They were Spirit-induced experiences that had no earthly explanation to them. From my years of being in the kingdom of God, I have found others who have had similar experiences. In this chapter, I will share some of these experiences in as much detail as possible. In some cases, there aren't words to express them.

# Chapter 11
# SUPERNATURAL EXPERIENCES

I drove home one afternoon in the summer, and as usual, I thought about things my heavenly Father had done for others and me. The next minute I found myself standing on the Mount of Olives facing the East Gate into the Old City of Jerusalem. At first, I thought this couldn't be happening to me. I was driving, but it was happening. Then the Lord said, "Turn your head and look over to the Valley of Armageddon." As I turned, a huge earthquake happened, and the earth split underneath me. My feet started the opening in the ground. Then the Lord said for me to prophesy these words: "You will be joined by another, and I will send the two of you to the four corners of the earth to tell of My coming."

Just then, I saw the other person standing next to me with a puzzled look on his face like, "I'm sure I had on mine." Together, we proclaimed the words the Lord had given both of us. As we spoke the words, the entire earth shook.

Then, I was back in my car, and a tremendous welling up inside of me caused me to sing out loud in a tongue I had never heard before or since. I had so much love pouring out of me that I couldn't stand it. I wanted to get out of my car and run alongside it.

You can say I never left my car, had a vision, or a dozen other things, but I know what I know, and it did happen. When I got home and was about to tell my wife about the experience, my mouth would not say the words. Over the years, I have tried to tell people but could not get the words out.

I happened to be in another church when a man came up to me and asked me what I had for him from the Lord and what I saw in him. I was so shocked that I didn't know what to say. I told him that I didn't have anything for him. The reason I was so shocked is because it was the same man who stood on the Mount of Olives with me the day the Lord took me there.

After this happened, I was so overwhelmed I told the Lord that He must be mistaken because I was the biggest screw-up and hadn't been able to accomplish anything for Him. The Lord told me that was why I was His best choice because I understood that I could do nothing without Him.

That happened in 1972, and to this day, the Lord has released me to share this with only one other person, and he has never spoken to me since. So hopefully, this is the right time as I do feel a lot of peace in sharing it.

You ask, "How do you know that you were taken away in the Spirit to Jerusalem?" It is because God had taken me up in the Spirit many times before that.

You say, "Well I have never been taken up in the Spirit and I'm a believer in Jesus." Then I would challenge you to ask your heavenly Father, who would never deny His children any good gift. Search out the God of the Bible and don't give up till He answers you in His way and time.

A friend of mine was distraught about never having seen angels. As we stood in the church that morning before the service started,

I prayed for him that God would open his eyes so he could see in the Spirit.

I was sitting about six chairs from him, and he was sitting in the chair next to the aisle. As the worship time happened, I looked at him, and he looked at me with such large eyes that I knew he saw the angels coming down the aisle next to him. He was so excited that after the church service he came up to me and asked if I had seen the angles. I asked him to explain to me what he saw. He said there were about ten to fifteen angels coming down the aisle about three feet off the floor, and they were dancing and worshiping. I confirmed with him that he saw correctly. He promised not to ridicule me about the things I saw from then on.

The only thing that prevents those who are in Jesus and believe in Him is our unbelief. I firmly believe that unbelief has been the greatest obstacle for the church, not the world, government, or other religions.

One man said, "Jesus, I believe; help my unbelief" (Matt: 9:28). All this man needed was someone who did believe to help him believe by showing him what he didn't believe. The state I was raised in, Missouri, is known as the "Show Me State," and I've heard that phrase all my life. Sometimes we just need to be shown.

I had asked the Lord many times to show this friend of mine what he desired. The Sunday I prayed for him was the Sunday the Lord told me that it was time, and if I prayed for the man, He would open his eyes this one time. He never again saw angels, but he didn't need to because he was convinced they were there.

Here is something you will have to set on a shelf in your mind for a later time to believe.

A family I had known for many years drove to their home state to visit relatives so they could share their newfound friend Jesus. They had a VW bus and had their three children asleep in the back as they drove along about midnight with no other cars on the highway.

## SUPERNATURAL EXPERIENCES

This was in open country with no towns around for miles. The wife alerted her husband about a car coming, and the two of them became concerned when it appeared it was on their side of the road. Here you had two adults wide awake looking at the same object coming toward them. At first, the man blinked his lights to let the other driver know he was another car heading toward it. There was no response from the car coming toward them. The man got over into the other lane, hoping to avoid the oncoming car. This was a two-lane highway with no shoulder to pull off onto. Just as the other car got within fifty yards of them, it swerved over into their lane and was right in front of them.

There was only time to say, "Jesus, here we come." Then a most miraculous thing happened. As they sat in their seats, the other car passed through their car. They told me this knowing I would have a hard time believing such a story. They said it was like slow motion as they sat there; they could actually see this happening to them. After the other car had passed through their car, they stopped and got out in time to see the other car's lights fade into the night. They looked their car over, and nothing was damaged except their understanding of how this could have happened.

When you search out the Bible, you will find that the things I have written down have happened in other places with other people. They have happened before; we just don't believe it when we read it.

A lady came up to me years ago and said that she read about a man in the mid-1600s, who walked around a town declaring that God would burn the town down if they didn't repent of their wicked ways. The man did this naked to demonstrate that we must come before God with nothing hidden. She told me that God would not let someone go around with their body exposed, and because this man was naked, it showed that it wasn't of God. I reminded her that the prophet Isaiah had done something similar, and she should not worry because I don't think God would call her to such a message. I think this was her greatest fear, and I reminded her that the town she referred to didn't repent, and three years later, it burned to the ground.

I was sleeping one night when I felt the wind go by. It was so strong that I could hear it whistle through my hair. I had the hold of another person's hand, but the wind was so strong I could not even turn my head; all I could do was look straight ahead. I could see an image coming toward me, and it had such brightness to it that it lit up a mass of people behind it. I thought there must have been thousands coming right to me.

We were close enough that I could see it looked like a picture I had seen in the Bible in the book of Revelation. As we got closer, I could identify the person in front. He was the King of kings and Lord of lords; it was Jesus. As soon as I identified Him, the dream was over.

You ask, "What was this?" I don't know, and I may never know, but it was God's way of preparing me for the destiny He had chosen for me from the beginning of the world.

You say, "Prove these things you have written and then I will believe it."

I say, "No, you won't because it has to happen to you for you to believe it."

There are times the Lord will take me to different places and show me things. One morning, I was praying as I do every morning, and I found myself in a bedroom facing a large bed. I noticed there were mirrors around the bed. There was one at the head of the bed, one on the right side of the bed, and one on the left side of the bed. There were sensors in the ceiling over the bed, around the floor of the bed, and behind me at the foot of the bed. Behind the head of the bed, I could see a vault with a very thick door. As I stood there, I recognized the person in bed; it was the new ruler of China. All of a sudden, I wondered if anyone could see me.

Then the Lord said to me, "Watch this." As an alarm went off, the entire bed was catapulted into the vault, and the doors closed and sealed as gas was released into the room. The next thing I knew, I was back in my own room.

If you want to check it out, you only have to call the Chinese and ask them if this is true. At the time, I was working for a Chinese company, so I asked one of the owners if they had been in the bedroom of the leader of China. He or she said, "No," and wanted to know why I would ask this question. I told him or her because I had. I described it to him or her. He or she turned pale, and from that time on, he or she would not come into my office. My job was at an end then, and it ended even sooner after that.

I was probably not using wisdom in asking the question, but I wanted him or her to know that any time God wanted to expose the plans of China, He could.

## Chapter 12
# PREPARATION

While in Bible college, I did a comparison paper between Buddha and Jesus Christ for a Comparable Religion class. Buddha was an interesting person because he believed in something he was willing to live and die for, but his purpose was self-serving as it only benefitted him.

His purpose was to escape this physical world to a place of total tranquility, or as he put it, nothingness. He could leave his body and travel to various places and then return to his body. He would tell his followers not to try this as they could get stuck outside their bodies and not be able to return. It is believed that if he would come to a river that was too deep and swift to cross, he would meditate and have smoke come out of his head and fire underneath him, and he would be transported over the water and then continue his journey.

Unlike the symbols of Buddha, he was thin. He had visited a friend, and they ate together, but Buddha contracted food poisoning and later died. One of the things he told his followers was they were not to continue their religion after his death because he was his religion. His followers rewrote his religion, and it became their way of life. They made a few changes that would then attract more followers. They began requiring the followers to financially support them. Funny how religion always gets around to having the followers support the religion instead of the religion supporting the followers. Maybe that's why religion is manmade and for man only.

Jesus Christ came with a message from God and continued to tell His followers that He did nothing except what His Father (God) showed Him or told Him to do. He preached that the kingdom of God was present, and if they would believe Him, they could enter that Kingdom now and after death. To prove His point, He allowed Himself to be put to death as payment for the wrongs of all mankind, so that mankind could enter the Kingdom now and for eternity. He told His followers that God the Father had given Him the power over life and death. To prove this, He was raised from the dead three days after He died. Over 500 witnesses saw him walking around, talking to people, and eating with them.

Jesus Christ told His followers to spread the message He had given them, for it would benefit mankind. He told them that He would prepare a place for them to live forever with Him. After His resurrection, the Holy Spirit was sent to those who believed in Jesus to enter them, help them in this world to tell others this good news, and perform signs and wonders that would give witness of these truths about God the Father.

Religion is an organization designed by man and taught by man to explain to mankind who "God" is or who He is not, but anything designed by mankind can only produce what is in mankind. The followers once asked Jesus why He didn't submit Himself to the elders of the Jewish leaders. Jesus said that the reason He didn't was because He knew what was in the hearts of men, and it was self-centered and self-serving.

Like Buddha, and many other religious leaders—past, present, and future—there are those who will try make you believe they are from "God," but examine their lives. Who benefits from their message and works? Who do they give credit to for good works? Do they do the work of the kingdom of God or attempt to use the kingdom of God for personal benefit? Who do they love? How do they show their love toward others? Do they constantly tell others what they need to do to be approved of by God, or do they tell others they are approved of by God because of the sacrifice His Son Jesus made for them? Do signs and wonders follow what they say, or are their words without life and power? How do they show compassion for others? Are they selective in who they show compassion to? When they speak, do their words penetrate your soul and cause you to want to know God the Father in a more intimate way?

My wife and I thought we would try religion once, so we went to a local church because my cousin went there. I sat there for over two hours bored out of my mind. I heard about the news that I could have gotten from the radio or the news reels in the movies. Everything was regimented and in man's order and liking. I knew I could do without this God, so I figured it wasn't for me, and we never went back. Besides that, my cousin was an "ornery guy" who showed no signs of having ever met God or even believed in Him. There was no outward proof that these people even knew God. They were hoping their good works would get them where only those who believed in Jesus Christ could go.

I do believe that these people were sincere, but they were comfortable with "their God" and not with **the** God. I once asked my heavenly Father what was the one thing that people were looking for in all these different denominational churches. He clearly told me that the one thing they were looking for was Him, but they wanted to tell Him how He could approach them, what He could say to them, what He could do for them, where and when He could speak to them, and what He could and could not do. In other words, they were so self-centered that they could not see outside of themselves.

We don't want to show up in heaven being a stranger to God. We want to show up knowing Him and His knowing us on a first-name basis. We want to talk to Him about all the wonderful times we have had with Him while on earth and some of the things He did through us to bless others. We want to talk to Him about the children who were healed and encouraged by Him through us. We want to rejoice over the many people He redeemed from death through us. We want to discuss the various wars we fought over the freedom of the souls that were brought from darkness into His light. We want to celebrate the hope we gave to those without hope. I could go on for many days telling you about all the things our heavenly Father has done for so many people, and He did it for you too.

I was part of an organization that tried to reach young college students with the message of the gospel. It was a religious group that did a lot of work in the late sixties on college campuses across the United States. I was part of the lay leadership that reached out to young married couples. I was at the headquarters building one day and met this young man that struck me as someone I looked like before I met Jesus.

He was good-looking in appearance but had some light in his eyes, so I knew he was a believer. He was new and had not met anyone he connected with as yet, so Jesus provided me for him. I asked him to tell me his story so I could get to know him, and he could express his change in lifestyle. I'll relay his story to you as he told it to me. I checked out his story by talking to others who verified it. Let's call him Larry for identifying purposes.

Larry was a fatherless boy in Anaheim, California, and was raised by his mother who tried to provide for four children, Larry being the youngest. He was an outgoing boy and made friends easily. Because his mother had to work, he was home alone a lot as his siblings were older and, more or less, on their own. One day, he met this guy on a motorcycle who had this neat jacket on and looked like a pirate. The guy took a liking to him, and they would go riding on his motorcycle.

One night, Larry was home with his mother, and the pirate came by and asked his mother if Larry could go with him to meet some of his friends. The mother, wanting her son to have a male to talk to, said yes. So, Larry and the pirate left for the meeting. When they arrived at this building, he noticed that there were a lot of pirates there, and they liked the guy that Larry was with. Little did he know he was about to be inducted into the Hells Angels, and the guy he was with was the leader.

He said there was only about eleven of them at the time, and they went into the building, sat in a circle, and asked their master to come and visit them. They called this master Satan. He said it was quiet, and nobody said anything.

All at once, a dark figure appeared in the middle of the circle and gave instructions to those there. The guy he was with said to him after the meeting that Satan approved of him because he included him in their plans, and he should never tell anyone outside of their group anything he heard. They had a name for the young members. I can't remember it now as it has been thirty-some years since I had this conversation with Larry. Larry said that each week he would go with his friend to these meetings, and each time, Satan would show up and give out instructions to the growing group.

One night after the meeting, Larry's friend told him that he needed his own motorcycle and would get him one the next day. About noon the next day, Larry's friend showed up, and they went looking for Larry's new motorcycle. They drove to another town and came to a group of motorcycles sitting on the street, and Larry's friend said he saw the bike for him. He told him to wait with his bike down the street and would be back with Larry's new motorcycle.

Sure enough, here he came with the bike, and he and Larry rode off on their bikes. He said he never dreamed that his friend just took the bike from someone else. Then they took it to his friend's bike shop and converted it into something called a road hog. It was great. Larry was not even sixteen, he had no license, and now he had his own motorcycle.

The following week when the group met, they discussed what they had done about the instructions Satan had given them the week before. It was the first time Larry was listening, and what he heard was not good. They had carried out a murder of a witness who was going to testify against some political leader in court. They talked about how this witness's life had ended abruptly, and everyone laughed. It hit Larry now that he was in a death squad who carried out instructions for Satan on people against Satan's work.

Larry's mother tried to get Larry to tell her where he was going and what he was doing, but Larry knew if he told her that, she might be killed.

Larry was now in the inner circle, and he watched over the next five years as the group grew so large that they now had circles in other towns and states. His friend's bike shop had grown quite large and was expanding into other states.

Drug money financed all of it. The group had taken over the drug trafficking in all of California. More people showed up at the circles. Politicians from all over the country came with requests, and they were willing to pay lots of money if the group would do what they wanted done.

Larry's mother tried to get Larry to go to this big meeting at the Anaheim Stadium to hear this man named Billy Graham speak about God. Larry asked his mother if the man was going to talk about Satan as well. His mother said that he did mention Satan at times. Larry thought it would be alright since he spoke of his master as well, so he went. During the meeting, the speaker said something he had never heard before. He said that Satan was a liar and murderer who wanted to destroy people, and Jesus Christ wanted to help people and give them life. This was news to Larry, and he wanted to let his friends know so they wouldn't destroy themselves because he really cared for them.

The next day, the circle met, and Larry was excited about this good news for the group. As they met, Satan showed up and issued his instructions to the group. Larry couldn't hold back any longer, so he spoke up and explained to the group how Satan wanted to destroy them and how Jesus Christ could help all of them live. Larry was then beaten and left for dead in a garbage dumpster.

Some homeless people found him the next day and got hold of the medics, who got hold of his mother. Larry's ribs were broken, he had a concussion, his left arm was broken, and his throat had been cut. Fortunately, his jugular was not cut, and a transfusion replaced the lost blood. Larry told his mother that he wanted to go back to hear the man at the stadium. On the last night of the meetings, she took him one more time.

When the man asked those who wanted to know Jesus to come down front, Larry, with his mother's help, made it down there. The next day, a police officer came to see Larry about his beating. After hearing Larry's story, the police officer said that Larry needed to get out of town and in hiding for a while because if this group knew he was alive, they would send killers after him. The police officer said he had heard of an organization who was working with young people on college campuses, and he would take him there because the group he had been in would come soon to pay their respects to his mother for the loss of her son. She was to tell them that she had him cremated and thank them for their concern. The officer told the mother that he couldn't tell her where he was taking Larry. He told her that if she valued his life, she would not try to contact him for at least a year.

Larry was at this organization for a year. After that, he was given a position in a church to help with the youth. The last I heard about Larry was that he had finished his schooling, had been given a church of his own, married, and had two children of his own. Now that is restoration, redemption, and a grateful man and mother.

We did some work at Berkeley University of California. There were some dangerous people there called the Black Panthers. They had put some of the people I worked with on a hit list. They wanted them dead. They knew they were followers of Jesus Christ. Several attempts had been made on some of the people on the list, and they came to our headquarters for protection. Our job was to hide them and get them to safety.

I understand that this Black Panther group was now openly operating in several of our states under the guise that they were just political activists trying to help the Black community.

I tell you they are of the same spirit as the group Larry was rescued out of. If we as a country are going to survive, we must fight against those who have sworn allegiance to groups like the ones I have mentioned, or we will become an oppressed people and slaves to Satan and his followers of darkness.

You say that could never happen. Well guess what, Larry's friend became the president of a famous motorcycle maker, and he is talking to other countries about bringing his company into their country along with the rest of his baggage.

Evil wins when good people do nothing.

## *Chapter 13*
# LEARNING THE BASICS

Having grown up as I did, I had no idea of how to be a husband or a father. I tried to find people I thought knew something about being a father and husband. I found a few, but after being with them and listening to them, I realized that they were just as confused about this as I was. I did the best I knew how to. My first daughter had the hardest part of growing up with me because I made most of the mistakes with her. Fortunately, she has a personality that is a fighter, and she fought her way through most of my mistakes. However, the two younger daughters still got their share of my mistakes. It seemed that as much as I tried not to follow in my father's footsteps, I ended up coming too close to doing just that.

My oldest daughter wanted a horse, and since we lived on five acres, I decided to build a coral and get her a horse. I found a couple who had a Welsh pony, and I thought this would be a horse she could start on. What I didn't realize until after we got home and surprised her with it was that the pony was green broke (which means barely broke) and had no training. My daughter wanted a horse so badly that she didn't complain. She rode the pony until it had its way so much that it wanted to be the boss.

I decided to help her gain back control of this little pony, so I got the pony out in the field on a long rope. I got my daughter on the pony and instructed her on how to control the pony. Well, the pony decided it had enough of this and started bucking. My daughter

Fell off the horse and landed hard on the dirt. What do you do when you fall off a horse? You get back on. She got up, and I encouraged her to get back on the pony and show it who was boss. The pony bucked her off again, and this time, hurt her arm, so I got the pony back to the house and put a bridle on it.

Then I got on it, as I had ridden horses most of my young life and even helped to break a few. The pony ran out into the street and dumped me off onto my back on the pavement. This made me mad, and I got on it, and we went around and around in the front yard, front porch, and back out in the street. This went on for about thirty minutes, and I decided I was not getting anywhere with this pony and needed to get rid of it and get another horse for my daughter. I found someone who wanted to take the pony off my hands, and I sold it to them for one hundred dollars.

I found another guy who had a nice Indian Paint pony. It was a little bigger than the Shetland pony, so I bought it. My daughter was happy with this one because she could take her friend on the horse and ride all over the town we lived in.

We soon became the Ma and Pa Kettle house of the neighborhood. We had three ducks, a dog, a horse, rabbits (too many to count), a hamster, and mice in the basement of the house because of storing the horse's food there.

I learned how to be a father through every-day experiences. Raising girls was much harder than raising boys. I could have learned easier on boys having been one, but girls were a completely new deal for me.

This was the beginning of learning how to be a father. When we lived in Highland, California, there was a family who lived about three houses up from us with three boys and a girl. When we moved to

Yorba Linda, California, we lost contact with them until one day, the mother with the thirteen-year-old daughter and the twelve-year-old son showed up at our house. We were entertaining the boy and girl when we realized the mother had left. She had given a letter to one of my girls to give to us when she was gone. The letter read something like this.

*Dear Bob and Sue,*

*My husband and two boys have gone back to Michigan and left us because we didn't want to go back. I have no place to keep these two children and no way to care for them at this time. Please keep them. When I get set up so I can care for them, I will return for them.*

Here I was—with five children to father. How do you become a father to kids whose father and mother have abandoned them? Having been abandoned myself, I could see the difficulty I would have soon. The girl was thirteen years old, and the boy was twelve years old. They were deeply hurt and felt like they had no value.

The hardest part was to get through the anger. When I ran with the kids on the street, it was the anger that was the hardest to deal with, and I knew it would be the same here. Each one had a sack of clothes, and everything they owned was in those two sacks. I was fortunate that the girl was about the same size and age as my oldest daughter, so they shared clothes, and the boy was easy to clothe. As a family, we were learning the real value of family and friends.

The boy had called his father in Michigan one day to ask if he could go with him. The father told him that he would send him an airline ticket. Three weeks later, a ticket came for the boy, and he went home with his dad.

## LEARNING THE BASICS

The girl wanted to stay in California, so she stayed with us for six months. She attended high school and became part of our family. I treated her like one of our own, which meant she got the good with the bad just like my own girls. We had our showdown over authority, and I didn't let her get away with her anger and rebellion. She didn't like it, but she knew I cared about what happened to her. Sometimes just having someone who cares is enough.

The mother showed up after six months for the girl. I hated to see her leave because I suspected her mother was up to no good. Once in a while, the girl showed up in our lives but only for a short time, and then she'd be gone again. The mother died alone and bitter at the world and everyone in it. We all make our own decisions, but sometimes we need help in making the best decisions we can.

We all have built into us certain disciplines to help us through life. and we all need to use them. Among other disciplines, we have self-control, which gives us the ability to think through each situation before acting out and helps keep us from acting out in our anger and fleshly desires, but self-control alone can only get us so far. When we feed our fleshly desire for drugs and booze, for example, it takes away our self-control, and makes us vulnerable to anger and other fleshly desires.

There is one discipline, however, that is an inward power dependent upon a power that is not of the flesh or soul. You still must make the choice to listen to that restraint and obey it, or you can disregard it and act out in the flesh. If you listen to the small voice within you (I'm not talking about the voices in your head) and act accordingly to what it is saying, you can save yourself a lot of grief in life. I know it sounds like I need to be locked up with the rest of the loonies but read on anyway.

The young teenage girl who was given to us for six months had very little restraint in her life regarding anger and fleshly desires. She had these places of pain in her life, and every time someone touched one, she would react in anger.

One place of pain was that she felt helpless, and when someone would ask her to do something she didn't want to do; she would take that as having to defend herself. Anger gave her the energy and boldness to fight back and defend herself. So anger became her only defense. When I told her that she couldn't do something, it didn't matter what it was, she felt that pain of helplessness and immediately defended herself against me. The more I would press her to do or not do something, the angrier she would become, and more aggressively she would defend herself. This happens when a young person is insecure and feels there is no one there to protect them against harm.

Some young people with a more submissive personality will give in to the situation while other young people with aggressive personalities will defend themselves, even if it means more harm to them. They would rather fight than feel the hurt. After a young person has been hurt many times, he or she will either withdraw into him or herself for protection, or he or she will become a person who will lash out at anyone he or she suspects might hurt him or her.

This was where this teenager was at. If she even suspected that someone was about to harm her, she would lash out. Her rationale was flawed in normal circumstances, but on the street or in an insecure situation, it could save her from harm.

While in the Marines, we were taught interrogation tactics to use in case of capture. One tactic was to communicate to your captors that you were compliant and helpful to them. Of course, this would only work for a short time, and then you were to take the offensive and conduct yourself in an aggressive manner. Then you were to switch back and forth. All of this was to buy time to escape.

I have found that in dealing with some young people, you may be dealing with people who see themselves as prisoners. They are ready to defend themselves against being forced into doing anything they don't want to do, no matter what. Some will be compliant; others will resist aggressively or run away, either physically or emotionally.

Our middle daughter was compliant until she became a freshman in high school. Our younger daughter was resistant and aggressive from birth. Our older daughter was stubborn but not as aggressive as our younger daughter. Here you have three girls raised in the same household, but each needed to be cared for in a different way. I always thought that if you treated each daughter the same, they would all turn out the same way. Boy, was I wrong, and so was the leading child psychologist of the day. If you haven't raised a child all the way through life, then you still have a lot to learn.

There will not be a perfect family or friendship while we are in these temporal bodies of flesh, but there can be better families and friends if we decide to work at it.

**Bob with His Bride Sue**

# Chapter 14
# THE FAMILY

Up to this point, everything seemed to be going smoothly. Our oldest daughter was getting ready to go to South Africa on a mission trip. We couldn't believe it; our first child going out on her own. This was a new season in our lives.

Why couldn't she pick someplace where they didn't have the apartheid situation heating up? As if South Africa wasn't dangerous enough, before South Africa, they would spend a little time in Copenhagen, Denmark, another very dangerous and dark place. They would witness to street kids addicted to all kinds of things, and there they had drugs of all kinds being sold at tables in the park. Then on the way home from South Africa, they would stop in New York City—at the time, it was the crime center of the world—to minister to teens that were recovered addicts.

Here is this eighteen-year-old girl, **our** eighteen-year-old daughter, going to two of the most dangerous places on the planet at the time, and a third place that was dark and full of emotionally hard people. Of course, she would be with other young adults and under the oversight of an adult, but we still had our fears about it.

When I was a kid of twelve-years-old, I hitchhiked over eighty miles from my hometown to Kansas City with another twelve-year-old for the weekend and thought nothing about it, but that was me, and I was a street-smart boy, not my daughter, a girl who knew nothing about the street life in a major metropolitan city. Yet how was she to learn to be on her own if we didn't let her out on her own?

She called us from New York to tell us about some of the things they did while in South Africa. They went down inside a gold mine, one mile under the earth, down a tube-like shaft. She described it like every so many feet, the temperature would increase until it was about 120 degrees when they reached the bottom.

They attended a German evangelist meeting in a tent that held 90,000 people. My daughter described how all the Africans sang and danced on a warm night, and the smell was almost overwhelming, but the presence of the Holy Spirit was so much stronger that no one minded the smell. She said that demons came out of people with a great shout, and the people wouldn't even pay any attention to it. They kept singing, dancing, and praising God. She said it was wonderful, and people were healed of crippling diseases right before your eyes, and they were transformed. The blind got their sight, the lame walked, the demons left people, and they were changed into new people.

After this, we were afraid she would go back to South Africa to stay and get caught up in a civil war, but she returned with the group she went and didn't go back.

She said she would stay in New York City to go out on the streets and tell all the people about Jesus. She couldn't wait to tell the pimps, prostitutes, robbers, and murderers about how Jesus wanted to see them all get saved. Surely they would receive her with open arms, or would they?

Finally, she was on a plane for California, and we were relieved. She was a young lady who had been out on her own in a foreign land and returned home safe and sound. I know you can be killed in Chicago easier than in Iraq; still, it's best that you're in your own country when it happens.

My middle daughter got tired of being teased for being a nice girl, so she turned to what all the other kids in her high school were doing. I remember the day she told her mother she was pregnant. It literally broke our hearts to hear this because we had such high hopes for our girls, and now we faced a grandchild and a seventeen-year-old daughter who would be a mother herself. I remember we were all at the dinner table, and I told everyone we were going to love our daughter and the child, no matter what. My daughter would not give the name of the father. She decided to finish high school by studying at home and taking the GED test for her diploma, which she did. She also decided to get jobs she could do at home to help support her baby, and she did well at it. She also decided to give the child up for adoption the day he was born.

As parents and now grandparents, we had a hard time with this, but in California, she could make the decision, and we couldn't do a thing about it. The big day came, and we went to the hospital to see our first grandchild come into the world and leave us the same day. It was a sad day for us. I remember going with a friend of mine afterward to pray for another couple's baby that was born prematurely and having trouble with his lungs. I was thinking here my daughter gave birth to a healthy boy, and we gave him away. Now I was going to pray with a couple who gave birth to a boy with underdeveloped lungs, and they desperately wanted to keep him. The couple's boy was healed, but I had lost a grandson, and we would never see him again. Sometimes life doesn't make sense.

My wife and I were at the beach one morning having breakfast when I noticed these boys about two years old playing, and the thought went through my mind, *One of these boys could be my grandson in a couple of years, and I wouldn't even know it.*

I decided then to talk to my daughter about getting our grandson back. I took her out to lunch the next day and told her about my life experiences. She then told me she had times when she was sure she heard her son crying and would even look around the house to see if he was there. Together, we decided to get him back. In the state of California, a mother has a year to change her mind when giving up a child for adoption.

She called the adoption lawyer and arranged for us to go to the parents' house and pick up our grandson. We arrived at the new parents' house, and all the neighbors picketed in front of their house with their babies in strollers. They had signs saying things like Indian givers and such. The sheriff's deputy was there, and we didn't know what to think, but we were there to get back our grandson and my daughter's son back.

We went into the house and talked to the adopting parents who did not want to give up this beautiful boy. I felt bad for them and everyone involved. Finally, the adoption lawyer said it was time for us to take the boy and my daughter and leave. We had to pull him out of the adopting mother's arms. We left immediately and made our way through the picketers outside.

On our way home, we had our grandson but were hurting for the mother who lost the son she had always wanted. We all began to cry out to God for Him to give this mother a child soon. We later learned that shortly after we got our grandson back, the adopting parents had received a baby girl and were very happy.

I had learned that being a grandfather was a lot like being a father. You were committed to raising your grandchildren as much as your own children. After several years of being a father, I finally learned how to be a father, and I realized I would never stop learning how to be a father. At this time, I have seven grandsons, four granddaughters, two granddaughters-in-law, and one grandson-in-law. Our family has expanded, and my capacity to love has increased along with it.

We had our three daughters and all their children with us at an amusement park one day. I took my wife's hand, stopped behind all of them, and I said to her, "See what we have done; isn't it beautiful?"

Life is so precious. How could anyone want to take another's life without cause? That is the greatest act of selfishness. Doesn't our life belong to the Giver of life? Doesn't the Giver of life have the right to choose what He would do with our life? How can another human being decide whether another person, who has done nothing wrong, deserves death simply because someone doesn't want to care for him or her? How selfish we have become in a country where we have everything but the value of human life.

Our youngest daughter was born with a determination to do what she wanted and wouldn't take anyone else's advice if it differed from hers. At twelve years old, she would stand toe to toe and nose to nose with me and tell me what she would do. It wasn't pretty when you had two determined people squared off at each other. I always wondered where she got that trait from until my wife said to look in the mirror.

All of my daughters were bright. Not one of them liked school. Of course, I didn't either, so why should I expect them to? It's that you want your children to do well and have a better start in life than you did, but not all children want that.

My youngest had decided to go to Colorado and work on a dude ranch for the summer with a friend of hers. She enjoyed the work, but at the end of the summer, she was ready to come home, and we sent her money for a bus ticket home.

She made a couple of other trips and decided to go to a cosmetology school. She then met this guy who she thought was a good guy and became pregnant by him. At this time, she thought that getting married was a waste of time and a piece of paper didn't mean much. They moved in together, and we had a new grandson with another daughter who wasn't married.

She was the most critical toward her sister when she was in the same position, but somehow, because it was her and she was older, it was ok. It wasn't that we disliked the guy she was with, but I could see differences in their relationship that would not allow this relationship to grow and become better.

I got a call from my daughter one day; she and her son were at her house and she and this guy she lived with were fighting. I got over there and found my grandson just wandering around in the driveway by himself crying. He saw me and came over with his arms up. I picked him up and put him in my car. Just then, my daughter showed up, and I got her in the car. Her boyfriend then showed up, and he did not do much of anything, so I drove off with my daughter and grandson.

Later, I sat down with the two of them and explained that you had to have certain elements in a relationship for it to grow. They didn't respect each other, they didn't value some of the same things, and they were both self-centered and self- serving. None of these things would allow for a good relationship.

She then moved back with us so she could finish her schooling. She completed her schooling in two years and received an AA degree from college. She was first in her graduating class and loved the work.

Here I was again with another grandson to raise after having my middle daughter's son living with us for over two years before she got married. I was getting used to raising boys, and it was easier than raising girls.

My younger daughter has been in the hairdressing business now for some years and has done well. I'm proud of the way she has worked and taken care of her son. He is twelve years old now and every bit of a great young man. When he was three, he started hitting golf balls in our backyard. When he was nine, I started taking him golfing with me. I had a golf pro look at him when he turned eleven, and the pro said that if he continued playing, he wanted his autograph when he turned fifteen. He has all the natural ability for sports like many of my grandsons and granddaughters do.

With my youngest daughter, I have learned to help and give advice only when asked. It doesn't help when I volunteer either. God, the ultimate Father, is a good teacher if we are patient and open to learning.

I had been told by people who were supposed to know how to raise a family, how I should run my family for the best results. What I have learned is that America has lost the understanding of how to raise a family. The most damaging institution to the family has been the social programs taught in and out of the public school system. I remember my girls telling me some of the things their teachers taught them at school. I thought they were exaggerating. I couldn't believe a schoolteacher could have so little wisdom to teach something like children suing their parents if they didn't like what their parents were doing. I thought my girls were just telling me something to make me let them do more of what they wanted to.

I finally went to their high school to talk to the principal about some of these issues. I found out that the principal was all for such teachings. I also found out that this guy was a lunatic, and I told him so. He laughed and said I couldn't do anything about it.

I pulled my two daughters out and put them in a private school. Their grades went up by two grades, and they were doing great. After several months, they said they would do better if we would let them go back to public school. I let them go back if they would keep their grades up. To this day, I regret making this decision because there is more to school than grades.

I thought if I was a better parent than my parents, my children would do better than I did. Boy, was I wrong? Society had changed and became more like it was when I was a kid. I believe that after World War II, our country had imported college professors to fill the need of the GIs coming home to attend college and follow their dreams. What the American public didn't realize was these professors were socialists and fascists. They brought with them a teaching that has been the ruin of our nation.

In Germany, Hitler knew that if he captured the minds of the young, he could spread his fascist beliefs much easier than forcing it all at once. This teaching had permeated our education system to the point that by the time my girls entered high school, the teachers who went to college were influenced by their professors in those colleges. One of the things Hitler did was he turned Germany into a state of one crisis after another so he could gain more control in the name of saving the German people. Does this sound familiar to anyone? My second-grade teacher, who had escaped from Germany, explained this to me and warned us about people like Hitler, who she described as a fascist lunatic.

I find it interesting that our legislators choose other avenues of educating their children. If our public schools are so good, why would all our legislators send their kids to private schools? Wouldn't you think they would want their children to attend the "wonderful" schools they tell us are doing a great job of educating our children?

It seems to me they are more concerned with social engineering than educating our children. Why are they so concerned with what our children think? Shouldn't they be more concerned with what they know? Is it so when our children grow up, they won't know the difference between sound wisdom and foolishness? Maybe they have arranged it this way so the ones in power can keep themselves in power and shame them and their helpers in the teachers' union.

# Chapter 15
# COMING HOME

While living in California for over eighteen years, I had not had a relationship with my family in Missouri. One night, I woke up in the middle of the night hearing a voice say,

"I want you to go back to Missouri and renew your relationship with your family. Do this for four years, and your relationship with your parents will be restored."

The next day, my supervisor asked me when I wanted to take my vacation. I wanted to go back to Missouri in the spring because the weather was not so humid then. Two of my girls were teens, and my oldest was just married. The two teenagers didn't want anything to do with Missouri, so only my wife and I went back. We were one day away from leaving when my sister called and told me that my mother had a heart attack and was in the hospital. We left at 2:00 a.m. the next morning, drove nonstop, and arrived in Sedalia, Missouri, two days later.

My mom was transferred to Columbia University Hospital for angioplasty surgery the next day. My wife's folks lived in Springfield, Missouri, and her brother came to pick her up from my mom's house in Sedalia, Missouri, while I went to Columbia Hospital to see my mom. The operation went well, and she recovered quickly. I asked her if I could pray for her, and she consented, so I put my hand in hers and asked our God to heal her in every way. I didn't want to say out loud what every way was because she would have wanted to argue with me about it. Sometimes it's best to be a little quiet about what you're praying.

My mom was ten years old when the Great Depression hit this country, and she was the third oldest out of five children. They lived on a farm, and her father worked at the railroad shops in town. The kids were left to tend to the farm. Her oldest brother had left home because there wasn't enough food for him. He rode the rails as a hobo for three years after that. With the oldest boy gone, they now had just enough for the others to survive. I think this had a lot to do with why my mother may have been crazy in many ways, but I think this also had a lot to do with why she kept a generous heart toward some people.

My next stop was to see my father, who had been divorced from my mother for about ten years at that point. He was remarried and living out in the country not far from my mom. I went out to his place to visit him and had no idea how this would go. He married a simple gal, and I liked her friendly personality. I stayed the night and was to go to meet my wife in Springfield the next day. I was ready to leave, and I hugged my father and told him that I loved him.

It was like hugging a wood post, but the last time I had seen him, I had a fight with him, my brother-in-law, my brother-in-law's brother, and a family friend. I remembered having my brother-in-law around the neck with my dad between my legs, as I was looking at the other two, inviting them into the party. I was about to break my brother-in-law's neck when my wife jumped in and caused me to calm down. I had hurt my dad's shoulder and put a large bruise around my brother-in-law's neck, it was one of those times I lost it. I couldn't even remember how it all started, but I knew I would finish it. This was right before we left for California. I went by my dad's house after that incident and apologized, but not in a meaningful way. To tell my dad that I loved him was hard on me and on my dad.

I went back over to the hospital to see my mother and tell her goodbye. I prayed for her again and left for Springfield.

The next year, my relationship with my father was pretty much the same but much better with my mother and sister. My brother-in-law was divorced from my sister and gone. I should have broken his neck because of the way he treated his family and my sister.

The third year, I went back to Missouri. My dad was working at a state park in southern Missouri not far from my wife's folks. I went over one day to see him and his wife. They had an RV and were sitting around a washing machine doing laundry. We sat, and I talked as my dad said very few words to me. I talked mainly to his wife. I left and hugged him, but it still was like hugging a wood post, and I told him that I loved him. I could not remember hearing my dad ever say he loved me before. As we were leaving the state, we went up to Sedalia and visited my mom.

I would spend a couple of days with one parent and visit the other each year and then switch the following year. The next year, it was time to stay at my father's house and visit my mother. They both lived in the same town, but my father was still working in southern Missouri at the state park. I visited him there but stayed at my wife's folks' house.

This visit would have the good-byes to my dad and his wife in a public place where we had lunch in Springfield. After lunch, we were in the parking lot, and I hugged my dad. For the first time, my dad told me that he loved me, and he hugged me back. This may seem like a small thing to some, but my dad never told me that he loved me, and he never hugged me. I felt that his wife had a lot to do with it, but it felt good.

I left my father and his wife to visit my mother. She was starting to get a little upset that I wasn't spending enough time with her. I promised that the next year I would spend more time with her. It was a good thing as the year after that, she died. I'm so glad that my heavenly Father was so merciful to both of us that I had those last four years of her life to renew our relationship or, better yet, form a relationship.

I went back to Missouri the following year to see my father and his wife; this was year four that the Lord had talked to me about. I couldn't believe I was actually excited that I would see them and that we had the start of a relationship. The Lord fulfilled his promise to me. At my mother's passing, I continued to build a relationship with my father and my sister and her family.

My father passed away this last year at the age of ninety-two. The only person I have not had a relationship with is my younger brother. I can hardly blame him for not wanting to have a relationship with someone who treated him so badly in our younger years, but maybe someday. As for my sister's ex-husband, I haven't heard anything from my heavenly Father about having a relationship with him. Perhaps that is a good thing at this point. My sister has some very wonderful children who have their own families now, and I do enjoy seeing them.

As I think back on these visits to Missouri, I wonder what I would be like if I had decided not to go back for those four years. First, I think I would have carried some hurt and anger toward my parents and blamed them for everything negative in my life. Maybe I would have ended up bitter and disappointed about life. How would that have affected my children and relationships? I remember some of the things I got to do that I would not have been able to if I hadn't gone back. I realize that not everyone have or will have the same results as I did, but it is worth the effort.

I have listed some of them here:

I got to pray for my mother and see her reunite her belief in her Savior Jesus Christ. She did change some. Each year, I could see that change, and it encouraged me to continue seeing my father as well.

**Bobby with His Mom – The Younger Years & the Later Years**

I got to meet my oldest nephew who was born with a heart condition, which took his life at age twenty-six. I remember staying at my sister's house after she left her new husband and spending the evening talking to my nephew about my Jesus. I don't know if he ever made a commitment to believe in Jesus Christ, but we had a great question-and-answer time together.

My sister's youngest son called me when they had their first son to ask that I pray for his son with an intestinal problem. The doctors had to operate on this newborn, and it was a risky operation. As I prayed about the boy, the Lord kept showing me these intestines, and they were growing. I finally had to call him and tell him that his son would be fine and would have an increase in his intestines. The operation went fine. The doctors would have to go back into the boy's stomach later to reattach something. When they did, they found that the boy had more intestines than with what they had left him. This boy is now a great ball player and a blessing to his parents today.

Many years ago, my great-grandmother had chased a priest off her property with a shotgun. It was customary for the priest to curse someone who would do such a thing to them. Up to this time, my family had been prosperous in finances. After this happened, no one in our family ever became financially well-off, no matter how hard they worked. I told this to a friend of mine, and he suggested that I pray and break the curse. He had been a missionary in Indonesia for twenty years and had done this for several people. I did and went back to see my father and sister after this.

I decided I would see if it worked. I had never been able to catch a fish on a hook and line before. I thought if the curse was broken, then I would be able to catch a fish. My sister had a five-acre lake on her property. My father and I went fishing at her lake. My father tossed his line in and was not catching anything. I tossed my line in and right away caught a nice catfish. I baited my hook and tossed it in again, and right away, I caught a nice croppy. By the end of our fishing time, I had caught four fish, and my father didn't catch anything; before, it was always the opposite. When I got home to Lake Arrowhead, California, I went fishing with a friend of mine. Before, when we would go fishing, I never caught anything, but this time, I caught five trout and had the largest one. He couldn't believe that this was happening since he always caught the fish.

A friend of mine told me that I should ask my father to give me the father's blessing. I asked what that was, and he said I should have my father bless me with everything God had blessed him with. On my last trip back to see my father, I asked him to give me the father's blessing. He asked me how to do that, so I put his hand on mine and asked him to repeat this prayer after me. "Our heavenly Father, I bless Bobby with everything you have blessed me with." I don't know what will become of this, but I'm looking forward to seeing it (I need to do this for my children as well). A few months later, my father died.

I have a niece who is very thoughtful and kind. She is such a help to her mom and her husband. She has a daughter and a grandson. We were sitting in the garage with the door open, watching the rain and wind outside, dipping cigars in wine and smoking them, when my sister's daughter drove up with her son and her boyfriend. They were walking up the drive when I heard the Lord say, "Pray for the daughter and her son but not the boyfriend." I asked if I could pray for the son, and the daughter said, "Sure." I prayed that the son would be raised as one who speaks for the Lord, that his words would have a great impact upon all who heard them. Then I turned and prayed for my niece. She became so overwhelmed with emotion that we had to help her back into her car. After I returned to California, I heard that she threw the boyfriend out and is doing much better on her own.

The path we are destined for is not always clear, but everyone needs assurance and encouragement in everything they decide to do.

**My Dad, Sister Peggy, and Me (Bob)**

# Chapter 16
# MATCHMAKER AND LIFE

It was a time for a new season of life for my wife and me. It was our daughters' time to find mates and start families of their own. I thought this would be a scary season in our lives. I was working in the meat industry at the time when my oldest daughter met this guy. We had met him before at a home group, and I remembered him as being okay, but now he was interested in our oldest daughter. Now it was time to scrutinize him a lot closer.

He and my daughter started consistently seeing each other for a while. After a few months, he called and wanted to have lunch with me. We met the next day near where I worked. My wife told me ahead of time what he wanted so I would be prepared. I had time to call a few friends of his I knew and ask some questions about this guy. The answers they gave were good, so I thought it was worth listening to what he had to say.

We started with small talk and lunch. Then he asked me the question he came to ask: could he marry my daughter? I asked him about finishing college first. He informed me that they couldn't wait another year and a half for that. I could see his point, so I gave him my blessing to marry my oldest daughter. Up to this point, I had not had to pay for a wedding. I had just made an investment and was short of cash, but they wanted to get married in a few months. I borrowed a few thousand and gave it to them because they wanted to plan their own wedding. This caused some anxiety in me because my daughter had never planned a wedding before. As expected, the cost ran over the original amount.

The wedding was in July during the late morning and early afternoon in a church with no air-conditioning. There was an accident on a major freeway, and some guests were not able to get to the wedding, but other than that, it went well. I thought she did a good job planning the wedding.

They went to Jamaica for their honeymoon and rented a tiny house (we called it the Hobbit House) before they left, so they were set to start a life of marriage.

Just as we finished paying off the first daughter's wedding, it was time for the second daughter to get married. I had decided to get about twenty young men together at my house for a barbecue to feel out the husband potential for my second daughter. My second daughter showed up for the barbecue. She thought it was a barbecue for people helping with the youth at church. I thought this would be great so she could get a look at the potential grooms as well.

I sat everyone in a large circle in my living room and asked them to each answer a question. The question was to tell everyone who they were. I explained to them that I had called them to my house because I had two daughters that were ready to look for a perspective husband. At that time, my youngest daughter and her friend showed up and immediately disappeared. My middle daughter, however, was caught in the room in shock and without a way of escape. I learned a great deal about these young men, and one of them impressed me. By the way, one year later, the one young man who impressed me became my second son-in-law married to my second daughter.

Now I had two sons-in-law. They have made their own mistakes and have had their own victories just as we had, but not to the same degree. I realize now I could have handled things better, but at the time, I was new at being a father-in-law. Neither of my new sons-in-law had fathers at the time they married my daughters, so they have had a tough time being fathers and husbands. It has been a learning experience for all of us.

We still have one daughter yet to be married. She has found a good guy, and we are hoping it will work out for them. I wish I had been a better father by working at a job that would have allowed me more time with my daughters. When your kids are young and you don't take the time to develop the relationship with your children that you need to, it shows up in later years. I'm still trying to find ways to help correct this.

It also shows up in your relationship with your wife. We dated for about four weeks and became engaged, and in two months, we were married. I know she didn't have any idea of who I was, as I had no idea who she was. We just knew we were attracted to each other. Thank God we both became committed to Him before it was too late. On April 1, 2010, we will have been married fifty years.

In the first few months of our marriage, I went with some buddies to the county fair. My wife was pregnant and stayed at home. My buddies thought they'd have some fun with me and bet me that I couldn't pick up on girls anymore now that I was an old married man. This hit me hard in my pride, and I would show them. I took their bet and picked up a couple of girls. We were getting something to eat, and I soon found out that my mom was working at the place we were eating. I was busted.

I thought that if I could get home and tell my wife this "funny" story before my mom did, it wouldn't be such a big deal. Boy was I wrong! I woke up that night to my wife walking around our bed holding a rather heavy lamp in her hand and she was seriously thinking about where to plant it.

Our marriage has been a commitment to stay together, no matter what, and believe me, it has been "no matter what." I remember one time I was so frustrated over her not doing something that I stared her right in the eyes and said in my old, fleshly, intimidating way, "You can be replaced." After driving to work, I had time to cool down and realized that she couldn't be replaced, and I needed to apologize for my words that couldn't be taken back. I called her as soon as I got to work and humbly apologized. My wife is one of those people who doesn't forget these outbursts of words, so I knew that someday this would come back to haunt me. Today, if I would have said something like that to her, she would be toe to toe and eye to eye with me.

My wife's heritage is Scottish, Irish, German, English, and Cherokee Indian. She is passive-aggressive, which only means you get yours later. I'm German, English, and Dutch, which means you get yours now. This means our girls are well-rounded. It's a miracle that we ever made it together, and the first three years were the roughest. It was because I was a mess and knew I was blowing it but didn't have a clue as to what to do. So I just blew it more. It wasn't until that night on that country road when I confessed my need that things happened. When I heard that man on TV saying you could have a new life, I just knew that was what I needed.

At that time of our lives, the grandchildren started coming into the world. We loved watching them being born; we were there for every one of them, seven boys and four girls. This year, we have had two grandsons and one granddaughter get married. I was so privileged to have been asked to be a part of each wedding.

Sometime now, we will be rushing off to the hospital to witness our first great grandbaby being born. This is a lot of how life works if we will only persevere with God's help and love.

People have defined love in many ways, but to me, love simply means selflessness. When we value another person more than anything else, including ourselves, then we can say we love that person.

Knowing that you're valued is the greatest feeling you can have. To know without a doubt that someone would be willing to give up his or her life for you places a great value on you. To know that someone would give up his or her time to spend that time on you is wonderful because he or she has given up something that can never be replaced, just for you.

We need to think about how much of our precious time we have generously given to someone else. This is an act of love. When one of your children asks you a question, and you're busy, give them love.

We tend to think of this life as a place where we are born, live, and die and turn to dust over time. We are made of the same material as the rest of the universe. We are molecules, atoms, neutrons, protons; these are eternal materials. They do not die or end at the destruction of these temporal bodies of flesh. Of course, we cannot see these materials with the eye, but they are more real than these fleshly bodies we walk around in.

Have you ever wandered at how marvelous the human body is? The miracle of life from conception to birth each one of us goes through. I think of how complex we are made and how vulnerable we are to the elements we find ourselves living in. Each generation is a story with a beginning and an end with all the things that happen to us in between.

Wouldn't it be so much easier if our lives were set on a track like a train, and we just ran on that track with a smooth ride through life and a sudden stop when we ran out of track? We would want to have life to make sense and be pain-free with lots of good experiences and full of happiness. If it were so, then we would not make any changes from birth to death. We could expect each day to be the same as the day before. Our lives would not need anyone else in it but us. We would not have to make any choices. Our lives would all have the same purpose, and that would be to stay on the train track. Everyone's destiny would be the same; even though we may look differently, we would all be the same.

Some of you are probably thinking after a stressful day that this sounds good to you. Others having a good day would say this sounds dull to them. Looking at today, how would it look to you? Would you change anything, or would you try and keep everything the same? I ask you: Do you have the power to do either one? Are you willing to sit and go along for the ride? If you had the power to change your present life, what would you change? Would you change all of it or a part of it? Would you do a complete makeover of every aspect of your life, including your physical looks? Let's say you went back to your conception. What power would you have to change anything about yourself while you were being formed in the womb?

When I was born at home, my mother held me up and dedicated me to the God of all heaven. Did that change anything? Was there power in her words, or were they only words? If I had known growing up that my mom cared enough about me to dedicate me to God at my birth, would that have made a difference in my life growing up? Would I have made better choices? It seems that while you're young, you take everything on the surface. Later, after you have experienced life, you tend to think more about cause and effect in your life. Unfortunately, I didn't learn about what my mother had done at my birth until I was a pastor, so I will never know if it would have affected my childhood any differently. I do think, however, that there was power in her wishes as a young mom and that God honors the prayers of moms, and maybe it's because of this that God had His eye and hand on me despite the choices I made as a kid and young adult.

For one of my grandsons, I came up with a song because of the circumstances in his life that had a negative effect on him. I could see he was feeling like he had no value, and I didn't want him to think this way about himself. I wanted him to know how much we valued him and, more importantly, how much God valued him. This is the simple song:

"I'm so beautiful, I'm so wonderful, I'm so me."

We would sing this song whenever he did not feel secure, and it would turn his day around.

I was in a restaurant with my wife one day, and a waitress walked by our table. Every time she did, I would hear these words, "I created her to be a classy lady."

After about three times of this, I stopped her and told her that her heavenly Father said that He created her to be a classy lady. One of the other waitresses told us later that what I said turned her day around because up until then, she was having a bad day. What power do we have in the words we speak, both good and bad?

## Chapter 17
# DO YOU BELIEVE IN MIRACLES?

Things happen in our lives that have no natural explanation; we call them miracles. I can think of many acts I would call miracles. I'm listing them as I remember from my early years to this day. Maybe you can identify with some of these as well.

The miracle of transformation was the first miracle in my life, being in the large room of the church and walking down to the front to receive something. I had no idea what it was. This was a miracle for me. I don't think churchgoers realize what a big deal it is for someone like me to do this. It is a traumatic experience for a person who has no frame of reference for even seeing such a thing. It would be like a churchgoer walking into a crowded bar, getting upon the bar with no pants or panties on, and doing a hump dance. That's how traumatic it is for someone like me to walk down to the front of a church. Then on top of that, having people gasping for fear that a person like me would come to their church.

I happened to be visiting the father of a friend of mine in the hospital when a nurse asked me to go with her to see a woman who was bleeding to death. We went to the ICU ward, where this woman was hooked up to all kinds of tubes. She was very weak and had a gray color to her skin. The nurse told me that she had a rare blood disease, and there was no cure. She said that the woman would die because her body could not retain blood. They had given her all the transfusions they could without any response.

This woman was given only a few hours to live. She had a nine-year-old daughter and wasn't married.

I thought, *Jesus, this lady needs you.* I asked her, "Do you know and believe in Jesus Christ?" She responded, "No."

"If you died, do you know where you would spend eternity?" I asked her. She said, "No." "Do you want to spend eternity with Jesus in heaven and someday see your daughter again?" I asked her. She said, "Yes."

I took her hand, and we asked Jesus to come into her life and save her and her daughter so they could spend eternity with Him. She agreed, and the machines went crazy, so I was asked to leave.

I was back seeing my friend's father two days later when the same nurse came in and told me that the lady I saw had left the hospital the day before. She was healed of her blood disease. The nurse gave me the lady's phone number and told me that the woman wanted me to call her so she and her daughter could thank me. Isn't that cool?!

I was at a conference in Bakersfield, California, with some friends. There was a young man who had been badly injured in a car accident. He had his right knee operated on and was wearing a brace on it to hold it in place. A young couple came to me and asked me to pray for him. As I prayed for him, he jumped up, took his brace off, and yelled out that he had been healed. I tried to calm him down, but he insisted on jumping up and down on the leg with the knee that had been operated on. He got the brace off and started running around the church. It scared me to death. I thought he should take it easy and go see a doctor before running around on his leg. Sometimes the one healed has more faith than the one praying for them.

A friend of mine told me about a boy who had been stricken with some sort of a disease that no one knew anything about. He was getting excellent medical care, but the doctors said he had lesions on his brain, they had no medical reason for it, and they said he was about to die. She asked me to go and pray for him. I have prayed for many people in hospitals and homes who were "about to die," judging by their medical reports. Thank God, He doesn't read medical reports.

I went to the hospital that afternoon and was seated in a waiting room filled with young people who were there to visit this young man. A young nurse escorted me in to see him. There were all kinds of tubes running out of this young man, and I asked the nurse to explain his condition to me. She told me that he was in a coma and not able to move anything except his head. She said even that might be a nerve condition and not the brain signaling the head to move. As the nurse told me the young man's condition, I sensed a tenderness she showed in her care for this young man. As I watched her care for him and noticed that she did so in a loving way, I knew he was getting the best of care.

I stood beside his bed and asked my heavenly Father what His plans were for this young man. As I looked around the room, I didn't see any signs that he was about to die, so I had to assume he would live. I prayed that his heavenly Father would begin this boy's restoration so he could return to his family whole and normal in every way and even better than before. Just then, a young couple came in, so I left.

A couple of days later, I called my friend and asked her how the young man was doing. She said the doctors said that it looked like his brain was liquefying, and they saw no hope for him. I told her that I thought our heavenly Father would restore this young man, and I would keep dropping in on him.

A day later, I was in the area, so I went in to see him. There were two nurses in his room when I got there. They were both young and had the same spirit of care for this young man that the previous nurse had. I waited while they finished caring for him. While I waited, I asked them questions about his condition. They told me that there was no hope for him, and the doctors told them that it was a matter of hours before he would die.

Again, I asked our heavenly Father about the boy. I got the same message to look around and read the signs. I saw no signs that he would die, so I continued to pray for his full recovery. This time, I noticed that he moved his big toe. I asked the nurses if that was him or a nerve causing it. They assured me that it was a nerve as he was totally paralyzed. I also noticed as I stood there praying that his eyes would open at times and then close. I asked the nurses what that meant, and they said they didn't know. He hadn't done that before. I left him one of my books on top of his headboard and left. I was so certain that God would heal this boy that if he woke up, I wanted him to have something to read or something someone could read to him that would encourage him that he would make it.

I called my friend who had first asked me to go see the young man and told her that it looked like our heavenly Father was ready to restore the young man. These were encouraging words for her. She was going to Ireland and would not be back for a few weeks. I told her I would continue to go by and check on him. The next time I went by was about two days later.

All that time, there was a large group of young kids in the waiting room who had come to see him. As I walked into his room, I immediately noticed he was moving one arm and one leg, but because one-third of his brain had already liquefied, the doctors thought that this was due to nerves and not brain function. The nurses told me that there were no signs that told the doctors that he would live. His father had made his funeral arrangements. Again, our heavenly Father told me to read the signs, and all I could see was that he would recover. I continued praying for his total recovery.

Two days later, I asked one of my grandsons to go with me to pray for this young man. He agreed, and we took some olive oil to anoint the young man for healing. As we walked into his room, it was clear that he was beginning to move more of his body. I asked the nurse about this, and she said that the doctors were going to remove all life support systems the next morning, and then he would pass away within twenty-four hours after they did this. I looked around and saw no signs of this young man dying, but what I did see were signs of his restoration.

This time, our heavenly Father told me to anoint him and call him back into his body. When my grandson saw the young man, he was overwhelmed by his condition. He had known him as a baseball player. I told my grandson not to look at the condition but to look for signs that our heavenly Father was showing him. We anointed the young man with oil, and I prayed over him with my grandson for his total restoration. We kept telling him to return to his body. As we prayed, the young man began moving a lot. The nurses came in, and we had to leave.

As we drove home, my grandson told me that he had never seen anyone in as bad condition as this young man. I reminded him again not to look at the situation with his eyes but picture our heavenly Father looking at him and speaking the words into him as we spoke them. Our heavenly Father's words are life, and when he gives us His words to speak, those same words become life through us. I told him not to worry, that the young man would recover, and we would see him at church soon. My grandson couldn't imagine that.

I heard that the doctors removed the life support from the young man the following morning, but he didn't die like they thought he would. Instead, they released him to go home, and every day, he was restored. Two weeks later, this young man was wheeled into church in a wheelchair, and one month later, I saw him completely restored and working out for baseball season. He recently gave his testimony in front of the church and was back to playing baseball on his high school's team.

Oh! What were the signs I was looking for? When a person is about to die, there are two to four angels in the room waiting to escort them to heaven. When there aren't any, it means the person will not die or is not a believer in Jesus Christ. I knew this young man was a believer. Another sign is seeing death on a person. It's like the person is gray-looking, which is not what I saw in this young man. On the positive side, another sign I get is a picture of the person looking physically restored. Now, don't ask me how I see these things—I just do.

*Chapter 18*

# WHAT ARE THE RULES OF PRAYER?

I'm going to give you a partial list of healings that point out that there are no rules for healings. Instead, there is one Healer and Deliverer, and He is Jesus Christ, the Redeemer of the world. Those who seek after the kingdom of God will see the signs and wonders He talked about in the Bible, not only the healing of the body and soul but the restoration of all of creation. The mysteries of God are hidden but will be disclosed to those who earnestly seek them out. If only we would believe the Creator of all things.

Restoration is a beautiful thing to behold, especially when it's you who's being restored. The examples I write about are simply a witness of the restoration that is available to all who would seek after the kingdom of God. I have seen the following examples with my own eyes.

At a retreat in Arrowhead, California, a young man asked me to go to the prayer chapel and pray with him for his friend, who wasn't in the prayer chapel, to receive Christ. I thought, wait a minute! We were trained to go to the person and lead them to Christ. The young man was so adamant about our going to pray in the chapel that I went with him. The next morning at breakfast, he came into the dining hall and yelled across the hundreds of people there that his friend asked Jesus Christ into his life in his room as we were praying in the chapel. He was so excited that he talked all the way through breakfast. Now the organization retreat we were at didn't appreciate him telling everyone how his friend asked Jesus into his life because it was contrary to what they taught. After all, they were supposed to be the experts.

Over the years, I have found it more productive in teaching people what they can do instead of how they should do it, especially when it involves things of the Holy Spirit and faith. The Bible teaches us why we pray for the sick, not how we should do it. We do it because of God's love for the person, and it's okay to give love out in any way you can.

At the church, I was responsible for handing out food for those in need. A lady and her husband made space in their garage to store the food. I was there picking up some food when the husband came to me in panic. His wife was in a coma; the husband had her tied in a straight back chair so she would not fall. She was not responding to any outside stimulus. She was completely lifeless, short of her heart beating. I reacted in a way I had never reacted in this situation before. I knew this was a battle for her life, and the fight was now. I cried out for God's help, and this still, small voice said, "Give her Jesus Christ's blood in exchange for her blood." When I prayed that, she came to and gained her strength back. By the time I left, she was walking and telling us she was healed. The following Easter, she got up in front of the church and told all of us that Christ had healed her, and the cancer was totally gone. Now this was a prayer of desperation and a fight for a woman's life. It was a heart cry to God to come and bring the power from heaven for healing on earth at that moment.

I drove home from work and had switched from one freeway to another. I was in a hurry and drove faster than I should have. As I came over a hill onto the other freeway, all the traffic in front of me was dead stopped. I had but a second to stop and knew I would not be able to, so I offered up a prayer, "Jesus, here I come," and closed my eyes. It was about a minute, and I hadn't heard any crash, so I opened my eyes, and behold, I was dead stopped about five feet from the car in front of me. I have only one explanation for this and that is God sent an angel to protect me and the person in the other car.

For weeks, this phrase played over and over in my mind, "Tell them they are a good church, and I am a good God. Then tell them that I'm in a good mood." Finally, one Sunday morning, I stood up in church and said what had been going over in my mind. I was surprised at the reaction of the people. It was like a revelation to them that God was in a good mood. Now I had heard another person say what I said, but for some reason, God wanted me to say it to my church. Sometimes we are called upon to carry someone else's water to a different place and pour it out onto the people of God. If I had thought of this, it would not have made any difference. It wasn't what I said that made a difference; it was that I said it. It was obedience that made the difference.

My wife and I were called to go and pray for a young man in the hospital. He had been in a traffic accident, where four people were killed. The truck had gas cans in it, and when it rolled, the gas cans opened and spilled out everywhere. The young man had been thrown out of the truck, and the truck rolled over him, catching him on fire. Another car had stopped, and a man ran over to this young man to put the fire out that was on him.

Every bone in his body had been broken. The doctors had to fillet him open from head to foot to set the bones. One side of his face was burned off, half of his ear and half of his nose was gone. His body had swollen to three times its normal size. All his facial hair was burned off, and part of his lip was gone. He didn't even look human lying there in bed. He was not conscious when we prayed for him.

We told the mother, brother, and friends that the doctors said he would not make it, and we comforted them before we left. Two days later, they called again and asked us to come and pray one more time as he was worse. I couldn't believe he could be any worse than when we saw him. This time as we walked into the room, he was able to look at us and say a couple of words. We asked what he wanted, and he said, "To live." We asked our heavenly Father for his life. As we walked out, I saw a picture of him standing in the back of our church holding a cane and wearing a black hat. I thought the Holy Spirit was showing me that he would live. One year later, I walked to the back of our church, and there he was. He stood there wearing a black hat and leaning on a cane.

He married his friend who visited him in the hospital almost every day, she is a wonderful woman. Several years later, they moved to Washington State, where he works as a technical writer. They have five children and still enjoy life twenty years later. At the time we first saw him, we would not have expected him to make it through the night. Again, it's not the situation we consider but the power of God and His grace in the situation.

A lady we knew came to my wife and me and asked us to pray for her brother who was damaged from an accident. She said that the doctors told him the left side of his brain was dead. He could no longer play his guitar or utilize other left-brain functions. We decided to pray for him with another couple for four weeks to see what God would do. After four weeks, we stopped to wait on what God would do.

The man started playing his guitar again and regained some left-brain functions. He went back to the doctors, and they told him that even though he could do most left-brain functions, the left side of the brain was still dead. How then can you lose some functions because of your left brain being dead and then regain most of those functions, and your left side of the brain is still dead? Go figure.

I hope you don't mind my going on like this, but these are the things that have shaped my character over the years. It is not enough that one says he or she believes in God. You must trust God and be obedient in stepping out and doing what He says for the benefit of others.

Recently, I was admitted to the hospital for some tests on my heart. I had just finished playing eighteen holes of golf and was on my way to my doctor's office to set up an appointment when I became lightheaded and felt I would faint. Then I had shortness of breath, and my chest tightened. I put my hand on my chest and asked God to keep me from passing out while driving to my doctor's office.

When I got there, I told them what happened, and they called 911 for the paramedics to take me to the hospital. They came and checked my heart rate. It was dangerously high at 220 bpm. They immediately hooked me up to an IV with medication to help get my heartbeat down; less than 100 bpm is normal. When they got my heartbeat down under 200 bpm, they transferred me to a hospital for more treatment. I told God that I had no idea what was going on, but I would trust Him through it. I was then transferred to another hospital and was there for more tests and an overnight observation.

The next morning, a chaplain came in to see people, and he prayed for me as I was going in for a stress test. He said he would be back later. As I went through the stress test, a couple I knew and my wife came to see me. We were all visiting when the chaplain came back. The chaplain was nervous, and he talked away.

The Holy Spirit told me to pray for the chaplain and tell him that he would be given an anointing to bind up the brokenhearted. As the chaplain rattled on, I interrupted him and told him to sit down so we could pray for him. I told him what the Holy Spirit told me, and the wife of my friend prayed for him as well. She didn't know him, and he hadn't said anything about his family life. When we started praying, she started telling him things about his family and life he knew she had no knowledge of. The chaplain was so taken aback by what we prayed that he could not speak afterward and almost ran out of the room.

The man in the bed next to me watched the whole thing. I could tell he was puzzled by what he had just seen, so I asked him his first name. He told me, and then I asked him if my friend and I could pray for him. He said yes. I told him what the Holy Spirit revealed to me about him. He was a lonely man with no friends or family, and he had a hard life of abusing his body. I said he was out of money and living in his parents' home.

Then the Holy Spirit told me to tell him that God would restore his finances and change his life of loneliness. He would be healed of his heart condition and would live to be much older. He was taken aback by this but thankful.

The nurse came in and told me I was discharged. I got ready to go home and left. I probably will never see them again, but that's all right because my part was done. People always think they need to see something change for their prayers to have an effect, but not always. There are times when months or even years later, I see someone I prayed for, and they tell me what happened to them.

We had moved from California to the state of Washington, and I had opened an insurance agency. A couple called me to come to their home and give them an insurance quote for insurance on their house. On the way there, Jesus spoke to and told me that this was not about insurance, and I needed to listen when I got there.

When I got there, the wife came to the door, and the man remained seated at the kitchen table. After asking them the usual questions about their house, I put my papers aside and told them that the Holy Spirit told me that this was about more than insurance. They told me the husband was a lumberjack, had been struck by lightning three years ago, and was not able to work because of the extreme pain in his lower body. I asked the wife to pray with me for her husband to be healed, and she did. We finished praying, and nothing seemed to change.

About three months later, the husband showed up on my doorstep to thank me for praying for him. He was completely healed and was back to work as a lumberjack. It's always good to hear what happens to the people you pray for but not always necessary. The important thing is your obedience to pray for those the Lord tells you to pray for.

Shortly after we moved to Washington, we moved back to California. Six years later, I met with a couple we knew from Washington. They told us that the man was still healed and working as a lumberjack. Did God move us to Washington just so this man could be healed? I don't know, but I do believe God so loves us He might do that.

As an insurance broker in California, I traveled all over California insuring churches. I must have prayed for over 1000 pastors, board members, and members in just about every kind of church there was. I asked my heavenly Father one time what the one thing people were looking for in all these different churches. He spoke to me clearly; "They are looking for me, each one in their own way." I approached each church with that in mind.

While driving to another appointment in Oxnard, California, I saw a church in the middle of a cabbage field, and since I had some time, I decided to stop and see if they needed insurance on their new buildings. There was no one in the office, so I walked around the building and heard people inside the meeting hall, so I knocked on the door.

Before this, I told my heavenly Father about the mistake He made by allowing a certain man to be elected president of the USA. You could say I was depressed over it and was whining to my heavenly Father about it.

Just then, a Black man opened the door and invited me into their prayer meeting. Everyone was on their knees praying, and the leader or pastor raised his head and told me that I was sent there with a word from God for them. As I sat there, I heard them praying for the new president of the USA. They were praying that God would bless him and direct him in every decision. I was so taken aback I started telling my heavenly Father how wrong and judgmental I had been. Then everyone got up in their seats, and the pastor asked me to give them the word that God had given me for them. I confessed to them that they had given me the word from my heavenly Father. I prayed a blessing on all twenty of them and their families and on the new president of the USA.

I walked out of there refreshed and encouraged. While I drove to my appointment, my heavenly Father showed me a picture of this new president in a church meeting, giving his life over to Him. Sometimes our judgment is the opposite of our heavenly Father's lovingkindness. I learned not to judge that day in a kind way.

**Bob after Catching Fish with a Pole**

## Chapter 19
# A TIME OF ANGELS AND DEMONS

You may ask, "Has anyone seen angels in this life?" I have written some things about angels but not in such detail as here. Not everyone in the church believes in angels. Sometimes I think more people outside the church believe in angels than inside the church. There doesn't seem to be a question about their existence; usually, it's more about their involvement in the lives of people. I'm going to tell you about the involvement of angels in my life.

The first time I believe an angel intervened in my life was when I was pimping for a cat house (brothel) on the other side of the tracks. I had an encounter with one of the prostitutes, and her pimp had gone out to his car to get a shotgun. I happened to be with two other guys, but they left ahead of me and were waiting in the car.

When I stepped out of the building, there were the pimp, his buddy, and the prostitute waiting there for me. I knew this was a life-or-death situation, so I decided I would act as though I had an army backing me up, and I threatened the three of them. I told them all the awful things I would do to them, and that surprised them since they had the upper hand. The pimp raised the shotgun up in my face, and I told him he better keep a gun on me because I was the most dangerous person he had ever encountered.

I saw this fear come over them as though they saw something behind me. Of course, I thought it was the two guys with me, and they had brought a couple of guns with them. The next thing I knew, the three of them put their shotgun down and backed away from me. Of course, I saw this as the time to press my case of threats toward them.

When they had left, I turned around, expecting to see the two guys I came in with standing there holding a gun or two, but there was no one there. The two guys were waiting still in the car for me and were scared out of their minds.

One of them asked, "Where'd that huge guy come from who was standing behind you?" I said, "What guy?"

They said, "The one that scared the other three people away."

I had no concept of anything that came even close to angels or God. I told them they were seeing things and that I bluffed the three people, and they ran off. To this day, when I think back on that situation, I realize there was someone behind me. You see, I remember seeing two men holding another man as one shot his head off with a shotgun on the street only a block away from where we were. Suddenly, it struck me that someone was watching out for me.

There was another incident when three guys I knew came by to get me to go with them for a night on the town. When I got into the car, the driver turned around and put a cocked .45 pistol up between my eyes and said, "Okay, Marine tough guy, let's see you get out of this one."

I remember thinking what I had done to this guy or one of his friends. My life flashed before my eyes in a second or less . . . Then suddenly, he laughed, turned around, and started driving. I thought this was strange because there was no reason this should have happened. I knew this guy, and I knew he could have pulled the trigger and thought nothing of it. Sometimes life is full of incidents that have no explanation. Do we have a guardian angel looking over us?

A commonly asked question is: Are there different kinds of angels? It has been my experience that there are many types of angels. Another commonly asked question is: Are there angels of darkness as well as light? I have not found angels of darkness, but I have found demons that represent darkness. Here are some of my experiences with these demons of darkness.

In the spirit world, you will find that it tries to attract you to its dominion, which is earth. When I began seeing angels of light, I also began seeing demons of darkness. I was in a home group one evening and saw this young man come into the house and sit down behind a friend's wife. It looked like he had a shadow over him, and it followed him in.

Then I saw this powerful demon manifest from him. That is to say, it was the young man one second and this grotesque demon the next second. I began praying in the Spirit and telling it to leave. It was a powerful spirit and defied me and my authority. It made the hair stand up on the back of my neck. I realized I had not run into a demon of this size before and needed help. I asked Jesus to come and rebuke this defiant demon.

As I prayed in the Spirit, I could see Jesus come, and the demon then cowered away, and the young man left the house. After the home group meeting, my wife and I drove home with this couple. On the way home, she told us that she had a strange feeling that night. She said she felt like someone behind her was going to stab her with a knife. The young man I saw the demon on was sitting right behind her. I asked her if she had that feeling after this young man left. She said no that it left at that time. This was many years ago, and now I'm better able to handle these situations, but never go against demons of darkness on your own.

You ask: "Can demons affect those who are in Christ Jesus?" Yes, they can in many ways. One is directly by attaching themselves to anger, bitterness, fear, and our family's heritage.

My great-grandmother was a little lady every bit of ninety pounds. She spoke mostly German and a little broken English. When my great-grandfather died, the priest came out to their farm to get the offering that my great-grandfather generously gave to the church. Well, the priest had not come to see my great-grandfather when he was dying, and this offended my great-grandmother, so she chased the priest off with a shotgun. Back then, there was a tradition in the church that the priest would put a curse on someone who would threaten him.

Up until this time in our family, we were financially blessed. My great-grandfather was a generous person, and everything he touched turned into success. After this curse on the family, no matter how hard anyone worked, we were never as successful as before.

A missionary friend from Indonesia and I were having breakfast one day, and I told him this story. He said that I should break this curse.

I asked, "If I did, how would I know it was broken?"

He said, "Is there something you have never been able to do?"

I said, "Yes, I have never been able to catch a fish with a fishing pole."

He said that would be the sign for me if I started catching fish with a pole that the curse was broken. I prayed and asked God to break this curse over my family.

I was in Missouri seeing my father, and we went fishing at my sister's lake. My father said, "Now I know you don't catch fish with a pole but give it a try." So I did, and I caught the biggest and most fish that day. I also went fishing with a friend in California and caught the biggest fish. The curse was broken.

There was a time when I saw so many demons that it distracted me from my worship, so I asked my heavenly Father to take away the demonic so I could worship in peace, and He did. Now I only see the demonic when I need to pray for someone. I do see the angels, and this is a blessing because they are from God. I have seen many manifestations of angels, and I will share some with you here.

Angels love joining in on the worship with the church people. They come dressed in garments or carrying things that are signs of what the Holy Spirit is doing in the worship and church at that time.

Some will come in dressed like monks of old with the robe and hood on. This is a sign of humility and humbleness that the Holy Spirit brings into the worship. When you see this happening, you will get a sense of reverence for God in worship.

Other times, the angels will carry a book or some other article that represents another thing going on in the worship meeting. I have seen angels come in holding a book, and that Sunday, there will be a revelation from God that is so powerful it can change our view of God.

Or they might carry musical instruments, and we would have an extra powerful worship time, where people were healed and set free while worshiping. There are times when small angels will appear over people's heads; these are ministering angels, and people are getting set free from all kinds of things that have hindered their relationship with God for years.

Sometimes there is a war going on in the heavens, and warrior angels will appear in a circle dressed for war. They will begin dancing a war dance in a circle, lift into the heavens, and open a place where I have seen the Lord Jesus Christ come into the meeting and go around touching people.

You may think this is too crazy, but how many of you go to the movies and see something more drastic and want to believe it is true? My wife has always told me that I have a great imagination, and I agree, but who gave me this imagination and sound mind to know the difference between what's real and what's not?

In the middle of the night, I was awakened to find myself between two beings or angels flying through the heavens. I looked up and coming toward me was the host of heaven with the King of kings and Lord of lords coming at me. When you can feel and hear the wind rushing by you and see that you are truly in space, can you deny the reality of it? I sat up in bed shaking my head at what I had just experienced. I have no idea what happened, and it has never happened like that again.

I am assuming that the two beings, one on either side, were angels but couldn't turn my head as the force of the wind kept it straight ahead.

Some other unusual events with angels were when coming into my house one day, it looked like an angel convention was meeting there. There were so many angels in my house I had to work my way through to my chair in the living room. I sat there trying to figure out why the large gathering. I recognized some of the angels from other times, but there were so many I couldn't count them. I sat there asking for the reason for the meeting. It seemed that it was a celebration of some kind because they were just a buzz, although I couldn't make out what they were saying. I decided to relax and observe what was going on. I guess they wanted a place to hang out for two hours.

When I have gone to pray for someone who is on their death bed, I have seen angels standing by ready to escort that person to heaven. There have been times when there were no escorts; I didn't know why. I remember telling the wife of a young husband that she needed to call those she needed to be there at her husband's death because the angel escort was there waiting. Sometimes the angel escort would be there one to three days before the person died.

There are others who have confirmed that I see angels as they have described them to me, and I was seeing the same thing. I'm not alone in this seeing of angels. A friend and I were putting together a men's retreat and were both praying that it would go well. When we arrived at the place of the retreat, we both walked into the meeting hall and at the same time, said what we saw in the way of angels and described what they were doing. This was great confirmation that the retreat would go well, and it did.

What is the purpose of angels in various places? What I have been given is that they carry a message from heaven to earth, and that message for me is in the way they are clothed and what they carry. Symbols seem to be big for me but may not be for others. Where do I see them? Just about any place you can think of. They are transporters of the deceased and for taking people away in the Spirit to show them things they would never see otherwise. There is not enough room in this book to list the times I and others have seen angels. Those who have must be careful to not become awed by them as they are awed by us who are in Christ Jesus. We should be careful not to get caught up in the worship of angels. We need to remember the One who created all living beings.

As for demons, they are the fallen angels who rebelled against God and were cast out of heaven to earth. They are not able to overcome those who are in Christ Jesus but can hinder us. They are still under the authority of us who are believers in Christ Jesus, but we are not to interfere in their work except when called upon by the Holy Spirit.

In the studying of the demonic, some people have been fooled into thinking these demons have more power than they do. There are religions that use the demonic world to influence the circumstances of this life. I have found that angels rarely talk to people, and I would question anyone if they declared such a thing. Not that angels couldn't, I just don't think God wants us to focus on angels or demons.

I think I have given enough to cause you to search out the purpose of angels from the Bible. The best teacher is experience. Even if it is only a one-time experience regarding angels, it is enough to recognize that demons are real and active in this world and to know what to do when encountering them.

# Chapter 20
# PEOPLE WHO HAVE INFLUENCED MY LIFE

A man told me one time that if I wanted to know how to influence people's lives, I needed to read about those who have influenced others' lives. This began my reading of over sixty autobiographies. I started reading autobiographies of people credited for making major changes in the lives of people.

## Charles Spurgeon

Charles Spurgeon was a preacher in England for many years. He was married, had two sons, and preached in a Baptist church in London. This church was so heavily attended that they gave out tickets each Sunday so people could get a seat. The building held twenty thousand people at one time. This was before there were sound systems.

When he spoke, his voice would carry to every seat in the building. One newspaper wrote that when the people would worship in song, it felt like you were being lifted into the heavens, and the choir of heaven was singing with the people in the church. There weren't any musical instruments, so the voices were the only form of music; it was awesome.

In Spurgeon's later years, he would sit on a couch and speak from there, yet everyone could still hear him. The newspaper wrote that at one time, one of the balconies fell through, and people were falling to the floor below. Spurgeon kept speaking, and all people didn't turn their eyes to see what was going on. The people that fell through the balcony gathered themselves together and continued listening, not missing a word. I think that is impressive that no one even gave any attention to the balcony collapsing but only to Spurgeon's words.

Every Saturday, people would line up for miles outside of the church, waiting to give an account of what God had done in their lives. Spurgeon would sit at the center of the church and listen as people gave an account of what God had done in each of their lives. He would have people there writing down each account, and on Sunday, he would read some of those accounts to the church at large. People had some amazing stories to tell of their experience with the living God.

Spurgeon gave an account of himself, his father, and grandfather that was amazing to me. His grandfather was preaching one Sunday, and Spurgeon and his father had come in late. As the two walked down the aisle to their seats, the grandfather would say a sentence, then Spurgeon's father would say a sentence, and then Spurgeon would say the third sentence. By the time they had come to their seats, the three of them had given the whole message. Spurgeon was eight years old when this happened.

He started a Baptist school to train pastors for the ministry. The school was offered at no charge to those wanting to enter a pastor's ministry. He was a man of great character and passionate for the souls of men and women. His life was an inspiration to me as a young pastor. He didn't focus of the manifestation of the Holy Spirit, but he never spoke against it. He felt it was not as important to him as was the saving of souls for the kingdom of God. My understanding is that both are equally as important.

We can respect someone for their good qualities without talking up their lack of qualities. We will only meet one perfect person while here on earth, and that is Jesus Christ, the Holy Spirit, and God the Father; these are three in one. We are given the ministry of reconciling the world back to God and not the ministry of judging the world.

## Oral Roberts

Oral Roberts was a gifted evangelist who had a tent ministry in the 1950s. I remember seeing him on TV in my high school days but never gave a thought toward him at that time. After I believed in the person of Jesus Christ, I read his autobiography.

At one time, he was ill and dying at home in bed. His brother came and took him to a faith healer meeting in another town. Oral was instantly healed and given a call to the ministry of being a healing evangelist. This often happens when a person is mightily touched by God through someone. Sometimes the person touched takes on the gift of that person in life.

He was so grateful for what God had done in his life he had to tell everyone that God could heal them too. He ended up traveling to towns that had no evangelist there and would put up his tent and tell people that God could heal them. People would come and be healed. It's simple to tell others about what happened to you and that God will do the same for them.

I was asked to go with a couple of brothers to their mother's house and pray for her as she was ill. While we were there, she told us about her sister, who was sick with cancer. Her sister was nothing but skin and bones. She had heard about Oral Roberts and knew if she could go to his meeting, she would be healed. The mother took her sister to the meeting with the knowledge her sister may die on the way there.

When they got there, the mother was asked to lay her sister down in another smaller tent. She said there were hundreds of people in the smaller tent that were too ill to get up. After the big tent meeting, Oral

Roberts came into the tent where she and her sister were lying. He was praying for people as he walked through the tent but had passed them.

She cried out, "Mr. Roberts, my sister will not live long enough to come back. Please heal her now."

She said he stopped and turned around and said, "Be healed in the name of Jesus."

At that moment, her sister passed this thing out of her bowels and onto the bed she was laying in. She said it looked like a squid, and the smell was overwhelming.

Her sister said, "I'm healed! Look, I can stand up!" And she stood up. She said her sister was still living and healthy. She said that the tumor that was sucking the life out of her was cast out of her. I do not question this lady's words as her two sons confirmed her story.

You ask how this can be. Some people have had others pray for them many times with no results. Was it Mr. Oral Roberts' words that made the difference, or was it the faith of the mother's act of bringing her sister to the meeting that did it? Whatever the circumstances, I say it was God who showed His lovingkindness toward the sister that made the difference.

It's the ministry of reconciling the world back to God. God uses every opportunity to show His love to people. You say God could have done this healing when the sister was lying in her bed at home. Maybe, but that is something only eternity will tell us. My belief is that all of these things could have been done while she was lying in her bed, but God had a plan, not only for this ill mother but also for her sister in taking her to the meeting. When you are a part of God's plan in a loved one's life, it has a lasting effect on you.

Both of those women know God heals even the worst of diseases. They both have a story to tell of God's mercy and love. At that time, this story changed my entire view of praying for people. Since then, I have had the opportunity to pray for thousands of people. I have seen wonderful healings that my most merciful God has done in people's lives.

## Kathryn Kuhlman

Kathryn Kuhlman was an unusual woman in appearance and speech. She was dramatic but in a natural or maybe supernatural way. She would stay behind the stage where she was to speak until she was told to go out by the voice of the Holy Spirit, then and only then would she come out onto the stage to minister. She knew the need to have God in front of her when going into battle.

She was dressed in a dress that would move in many directions at once. Her speech was over-pronounced as she had a speech impediment. If she spoke too quickly, her words would run together, and people could not understand her.

She told a story about why she was not married. I will attempt to tell it from memory here. She was one of the few women to be a preacher in her time. She was always under scrutiny from other people who didn't believe women should be in leadership in the church. People were suspicious of her since she was not married. She got tired of answering questions about these subjects, so she decided to get married and end at least one of the criticisms.

The Lord had told her not to get married as she was His bride and would not have time for a family in His plans, but she wanted to get some relief from the talk of others. So she got married, knowing it wasn't what she was supposed to do. A couple of weeks into her marriage, she had a visitor who gave her a message from God regarding her marriage. She realized she had made a big mistake and annulled the marriage. She made some mistakes but has always returned to what she knew to be God's will for her. She opened a house of healing in Philadelphia and began her healing ministry. In her autobiography, she tells of some of the healings God had done for people.

I remember this one story where a man brought his brother to her healing building.

While in his hospital bed, the ill brother was given a dream that if he would go to Kathryn's meeting, he would be healed. At the same time, the man was given the same dream, but his dream was that he had to get his brother to the meeting. His brother was so ill and crippled that the man had to bring him in an ambulance. The brother was brought in on a stretcher and laid in front of the stage Kathryn Kuhlman spoke from. The man was so ill he had to have a nurse go with him in the ambulance to attend to his need for oxygen.

Kathryn Kuhlman was given a vision while she was fasting and praying for this meeting about this man who would be there. Here you have three people in different areas, miles apart, being told the same message about this one man. It sounds like a setup to me. When Kathryn came out onto the stage, she called the man by name and knew his condition; she said he would be healed and restored to wholeness. Everyone expected to see this man rise up and walk or run, but neither happened.

At the end of the meeting, the man was so desperate he started trying to get to his feet, and as he tried, he was given new strength until he was standing up. What was so amazing about this was this man was dying of MS and was so curled up into a ball that there was no way he could have done this on his own.

I don't know if he needed to try and get up because there was no way he could, or if he needed to be so desperate that he would not give up on what the Lord had told him. I think sometimes we give up too soon and do not take by demand what God is offering us. Do not give up on God.

## Percy Gunthridge

Percy Gunthridge is a theologian of excellence and integrity in that he never held back from teaching what was in the text he was teaching from just because someone might be offended. Why, you ask? Because he has lived it. I met Percy at a family camp I didn't want to go to but my friend persisted that I should go. Percy had been a professor at Oxford University in England for many years.

One day while waiting for a bus, he had a revelation that changed his life forever. He quit his professorship at Oxford and began teaching and evangelizing on his own. Percy was to teach in the morning session, and I was to preach in the evening. Percy was a no-nonsense man of ninety-two years, and he didn't have time to waste, as he put it to me.

After I taught that evening, I noticed Percy seemed irritated. I thought maybe he was not used to my style of preaching. Percy announced that he would hold a prayer meeting the next morning at 6:00 a.m. for anyone who wanted to come. Since I'm an early riser, I went. Percy was sitting in an upright chair smiling at the five of us who showed up.

He started with a revelation and a short song. This puzzled me as I expected a long prayer. Then someone else had a verse they read, another had a Psalm, and I had a verse. This continued for well over an hour, but it seemed like only a few minutes. Finally, people kept coming in who needed to use the room we were in. Percy ended in a prayer for me. He asked God to anoint me for the evening service with revelation and power to minister. I appreciated it, and we broke up as Percy was to teach after breakfast, which we had missed.

As I listened to Percy teach, his revelation, knowledge, humbleness, love, and grace impacted me and everyone. He was truly Christ personified in the flesh of a ninety-two-year-old saint who I had never heard of. I thought, *where has this man been?*

After lunch, my wife and I sat with Percy and listened to the stories he had to tell us about his relationship with the God of glory. Before we knew it, it was time for dinner, but we were hungrier for his words of encouragement and the things he had experienced in his years in the kingdom of God. I had to get ready to preach that night, and I needed to prepare.

As I tried to put together the things I had planned, it didn't come together. At first, I was panicked, and then it dawned on me that I needed to be open to the Lord's revelation like we were that morning. I relaxed and began praying for the people who would come to hear something from the Lord, not from me. When it was my time to preach, I was ready and filled up with the Holy Spirit and revelation.

We had a great time that evening in ministering to the people, and afterward, Percy came over to me and said, "Now that was much better than yesterday." I thanked him for the prayer session that morning and the stories after lunch that encouraged me to rethink what I was about.

At the prayer meeting the next morning, there were over forty people in that little room to pray. Percy started out the same way as he did with the five of us that came the morning before. Everyone was blessed, and over forty people missed breakfast that morning.

That evening before I got up to preach, Percy asked me to pray for him because he believed God had a message for him, and He would give it through me.

He no more than got the words out, and the Holy Spirit said, "Tell him he has been promoted and will spend his last days as my prophet to the unknown places in England."

I prayed that way, and after that, Percy said, "That is what I have been asking for well over two years." He said he had not planned on coming to this family camp, but the Lord told him I would be there, and He would speak to him through me. Percy had so many degrees and honors I couldn't begin to list them here, but the one thing I was most impressed with was his honesty, humbleness, grace, love, and relationship with our God.

After that, I wrote him for a short time, and then I never heard from him again. I know he was true to the voice of our God wherever that took him.

"Percy, you were a breath of fresh air when I needed it most. I can't wait to see you again in the kingdom of our God. My prayer is that I can be half the blessing to others as you were to my wife and me."

This is one of the stories Percy told us that I need to relay to you:

I (Percy) was teaching in a church where I had been the pastor for about one year. Some of the deacons came to me just before a meeting and told me that we needed to watch out for a ruddy Scotsman. He had been shouting in churches. I started teaching, and we were all on pins and needles about this ruddy Scott who was supposed to come in and disrupt things.

This went on for a couple of Sundays, and then on the third Sunday, as I was teaching, someone shouted very loud. Everyone was looking for the redheaded Scot, and he shouted again. Then I saw him. He was sitting behind a post in the church.

I kept on teaching, determined not to let that Scot disrupt my church. Then something changed. As the Scot was yelling, I suddenly felt the Holy Spirit come upon me, and my teaching began to have power in it. As I kept teaching, the ruddy Scot kept shouting, and we broke out in revival. I asked the ruddy Scot about his shouting, and he told me that he was shouting the demons out of our church. I told him he could shout anytime he felt like it. The ruddy Scot stayed with us for over three years, and we had revival for the three years.

## Chapter 21
# NEW CHALLENGES

Entering the senior years can be challenging in many ways. One is the physical aspect of being older than you thought you would ever be. It's easy to put on weight and twice as hard to take it off. All the injuries you incurred at a young age, thinking they only hurt for the moment, come back and cause you physical hardship in your later years.

When I was riding bulls in amateur rodeos, I would get stepped on and limp away to work it off, acting like it didn't really hurt, knowing I had to get back on the bull. I know now that it really did injure me and caused me to need a hip replacement at sixty-seven years of age. Remember those times in football when you hurt your shoulder and got a shot for it? Well, later, it caused arthritis in the shoulder. Remember the time you hurt your knee in wrestling and later it caused your knee to pop when you get up because there's no longer any cushion between the bones? These are physical signs that you must meet some new challenges in your life.

There are mental challenges with memory as well. You can clearly remember what happened thirty years ago but forget what you went after in the next room, so you stand there waiting for the answer to come. You know you knew how to spell the word yesterday but can't remember how to spell the word today. You know you have a lot to offer to your family and country in life experiences, but your family and country think you're too old to have value in the modern age of today. They think you're not progressive enough, yet you have progressed more in your seventy years than they have in their twenty-some years. In fact, you know more about what works now than you did at twenty years of age.

Lessons in life teach us more over time than life lessons teach us at the time. It is clear to me that I could have done much better at finances for myself than I did. So I put together a CD on personal finances for my children and grandchildren. I tried to give them some truths that I had learned the hard way. I always think it's easier to learn a truth the easy way than the hard way.

There's an old saying in Texas, "Unless you have gone bankrupt at least three times, you're not a businessman." One of my greatest fears in life was going bankrupt until a situation I had no control over caused me to go bankrupt. My lesson learned was never trust a politician when he or she says he or she is going to help you make money. I learned that politicians don't make money; they spend money. Businessmen make money so politicians have money to spend. Today's economy is a prime example of this truth. There is too much resistance to making money by politicians and too much spending money that hasn't been made yet by those same politicians.

The system that our forefathers created isn't what needs change; it's the hearts of the people in the system that needs to be changed. What I have learned about people is that we do the things we have the power to do. The more power we get, the more we do what we are capable of doing. Not that what we do is always good or bad, but it's what we do to get more power.

When people gain more power, they forget that the power they have gained is to us to benefit others; instead, we use this power for our own benefit. Lord Acton put it well when he said, "Power tends to corrupt and absolute power corrupts absolutely." We become arrogant and proud, and then everything is centered on our power. People deceive themselves by thinking they are doing good when all they are doing is satisfying their own greed and lust. They lose their way in caring for others and only care about themselves. This is the self-centeredness of people's hearts, and it can become the greatest challenge in our lives. No one is complete when they no longer care for others.

It has become acceptable in our culture that when you have worked and given so much of your life, it's time to take some life for yourself. We give it a respectable name called retirement. To me, this is a waste of talent and wisdom in our country.

Everyone has more to give than they realize, and we should be giving it away to others so they can be encouraged to continue their lives in a productive way. It bothers me to think of people who retire and check out of life by no longer helping others, not even their own families. My challenge now is to continue to give not only to my children but also to my grandchildren and their children. My wife and I will always have plenty to do in our family, and when time allows, in the lives of others.

I think of people who travel around in their RVs and go to various places to get away from the winter where they live or go to a warmer climate. They leave their homes and family to go out and be free from work and the responsibilities they have had all their lives. After a few years, the RV has lost its glamour, and those they used to see on the road are no longer there because the circumstances of life have prevented them from going out any longer. Now because they have been gone for several years doing their own thing, they have missed out on events in their family life, that is, the birth of grandchildren, grandchildren growing up, important decisions their kids have been faced with, and so on. They have spent their last useful years on themselves and are left with only themselves. This is a waste of life, not living.

Why is time so valuable? Because it can never be regained once it has been spent. No amount of money can buy it back. Time is the most valuable thing we have to give, and we get to choose whomever we want to give it to, and because of that, it is most valued by those you give it to. Wisely spend your time here and give it to those whom you value.

Remember the energy you used to have when you were in your twenties and thirties? At sixty-five years old, we have the same energy we had in our twenties and thirties, but it doesn't last as long. My friends and I used to play thirty-six holes of golf in a day and sometimes another nine holes on top of that. Now I'm lucky to get around eighteen holes and still have some energy to spare. There was a time in the Marines when I could stay awake for five days and nights without any sleep and had to do forced marches every four hours to hide our location. Today, you would have to carry me after twenty-four hours and no sleep.

What happened to this body? When I look into the mirror, I see this young man in this old body, and it doesn't make sense. The other thing is when you start losing friends to death. In five years, we lost a friend every six months, and it does affect your attitude. I accept the fact that we are only here for a short time, and we must wisely use that time because we can never get it back.

I know people attempt to improve their body's condition. Some have cosmetic surgery on just about every part of their body. I see people who have had so many facelifts they almost look mummified. These are usually people who are in the public eye a lot, and it is important that they look good or young to others. There is a limit to how long you can do that.

I have a mile-and-a-half walk I go on when I'm not writing. I enjoy it as it gives me a break in my schedule, and I feel better when I exercise, but there are some days I just don't want to do it. I try to play eighteen holes of golf at least once a week and still enjoy getting out with friends for that. Sometimes we have a young guy play with us,

## NEW CHALLENGES

and we all try and keep up with him, then we realize we aren't there anymore, bummer.

My greatest challenge today is how to keep my relationships alive and active. I'm limited on time because my family is expanding; my grandchildren are getting married, and after that, there will be great grandchildren. Life goes on, expanding beyond our capacity to keep up with it.

When there were five of us, it was easier to give everyone a lot of Christmas presents. Then there came sons-in-law, and we were able to keep up with that. Then there came grandchildren, and we kept up with that. Now there are over twenty of us, and we are still growing. So, when you add birthdays and holidays for over twenty people plus your parents, which adds another six, you are looking at a challenge to just remember birthdays (we are starting to forget birthdays, darn it), graduations, and holidays.

Of course, you want to remember your friends as well, so now you're thirty-plus people. For us, that's over $3,000.00 a year, not including charitable organizations. I remember one year we gave out over $11,000.00 and only took in $10,500.00 because we were starting a new business. Now that makes for a generous heart or foolish mind. We love to give, and we receive back a lot of satisfaction because of it. It's what keeps us from being stingy and greedy.

I don't appreciate people who always want us as a nation to give more when those very same people give very little or nothing. I remember one year, one of the candidates told everyone how we should give to the poor. Later, it was found out through his own financial report that he only gave $374.00 to the poor the year before, which was less than 1/100 percent of his income of over $500,000.00, and that same person wants the whole world to give him money so he can improve our quality of life when he has already shown that he didn't take care of the people he was supposed to in the first place. Now that is greed and a scam in my book.

Always be careful of people who want you to do good for others when it only benefits them. That's like taking responsible peoples' tax money and giving it away to irresponsible people who can't pay for what they've already bought. Then they tell the people who received our tax dollars that the money belonged to the people who gave it to them when it came from you and me. Then they make sure those who helped them give out the money get paid almost as much money as they gave out as if they earned it; this is evil because it is a lie and greed. These same people then get together and tell each other how generous they are with our tax dollars, as if they pulled the same amount of money from their own pockets. Of course, you will never find out how they do it because they protect their own and not the taxpayer.

I have been an insurance broker for over twenty-five years, and each time the politicians tried to make the insurance industry better, it always cost the people more money for insurance. Why, you ask? Well, they changed laws that would allow more lawsuits so the lawyers would benefit by making more money, and then they would give more money to the politicians for making the changes.

The challenge at this time in our country is to work hard against those trying to take over our country by falsely creating financial crises to take more control of our lives. Funny, while they are in charge, they keep blaming others for the decisions they are responsible for and never take responsibility for their own failures.

*Chapter 22*

# IF I WERE PRESIDENT OF THE USA

Have you ever thought of being the president of the United States of America? What would you do in that position? I have thought of being just that and the things I would do.

The highest priority would be to create an atmosphere of hope. When people lose their vision for life, they perish. Everyone needs something to hope for to continue pursuing their purpose for existing. What would people want to hope in? The one thing we all need to hope in is something greater than ourselves. When we have only ourselves to hope in, we know that isn't enough because we know who we are and what we are capable of. We know from history how we have failed at giving false hope in our efforts at trying to give hope. We need hope that doesn't have the same faults we have. Otherwise, it will not sustain us in the difficult times, times when our efforts are not enough to keep us going forward. We need a hope that will let us sleep at night with a secure sense of peace, a hope that when all else looks the darkest, it gives us enough light to see our way through that darkness.

Where can we find such hope in this world that threatens us every day of our lives? Many people have searched for this hope; many have found it, but others have not. Could it be that all people have this hope available to them; they just don't know it? Every government has started by giving hope to people. Some have been false hope, and others have found real hope.

Our country was founded on such a hope that guaranteed all people would be given certain rights that every person desires to be treated in a just manner and have the freedom to pursue his or her dreams of a better life for him or herself and his or her loved ones. As a citizen of this country, I have inalienable rights to freedom, the pursuit of happiness, and equality under the constitution of this country. We call it the Constitution and the Bill of Rights.

This gave us the moral standard to do business in an ethical way and protect ourselves from those who didn't want to live by a moral standard. It was established so that the hope we were to have would come from something that was greater than ourselves. We identified that hope as God. Now after over 200 years, we have people who have been taught differently than we have been taught. The hope we once had is no longer valid. So, for over seventy-five years, we have slowly parted from our moral law and have given up on our hope at least enough to make a difference in our lives.

Let's see, now we have increased violent crimes and poverty, have no moral code, rebellion on all sides, no integrity in business, a crumbling education system, lost hope in our way of life, and are aimlessly wandering around. Our prisons are full, and our places of worship are empty, and we call this leadership!

This is the kind of leadership that leads nations to their grave. Is it too late to peacefully turn this around, or will it take a revolution like the one we had to establish this nation? Only 20 percent of the people fought in the revolution that established this nation. Maybe it will take that same 20 percent to reestablish it.

My prayer is that it won't take such drastic steps. No one wants another revolution, but no one wants to live under tyranny either.

What is the answer to our dilemma, and will it be peaceful? It's too early to tell at this point because no one has come up with a plan. I purpose a plan in the next chapter that I think would work. See what you think.

As president, I would order our military along our borders to stop all traffic illegally coming into this country. After that, anyone caught illegally coming into this country the first time would be immediately deported. Everyone illegal in this country would be given sixty days to leave this country in peace, and after that, they would be deported. I would also review all inmates in prison to determine if they need to be in prison. If they are from another country and are not here legally, then they would be deported. This would establish our boarders and sovereignty as a nation.

Some of you would condemn my harsh tactics and yet you don't condemn the tactics of the countries who purposely send their worst citizens to illegally enter this country. We have taken in Cuba's worst criminals, and no one says a thing, even when these very people kill our citizens and law enforcement men and women. I would abolish all sanctuary cities, and any city, county, or state government who does not enforce our immigration laws would be prosecuted.

My next step would be to drug test every person working in every position in our government, elected or not. Those who test positive would get a warning and be put into a treatment program. If they test positive again after the treatment program, they would be sent to a camp for treatment where they would not be able to get drugs. If after this, they test positive, they would be fired and incarcerated until they are no longer using drugs of any kind. The reason we can't stop the drugs in this country is because we have too many people in our government who are for the use of drugs and using drugs. This would take those people off the users list and put them on the enforcement list against drugs. Any foreign government that encourages the shipment of drugs into this country would be punished.

The next thing I would do is to clean up the voting process in this country. Only those who have ownership of property would be allowed to vote. The reason for this is if you're responsible enough to save money and buy a house, land, or business, you're invested enough to vote for the best interest of this country. Everyone would have a voting identification, and anyone caught illegally voting would lose his or her right to vote forever. If you have to invest or earn your right to vote, then you will be more inclined to value that right.

Every man and woman who reach the age of eighteen will serve two years in the armed forces; no exceptions will be allowed. If they don't serve, they will lose their citizenship. If you don't value this country enough to fight for it, then you need to find a country you can fight for. The best way to value freedom is to have that freedom taken away from you while in the armed forces and then have it given back to you once you have fought for and earned it.

I would abolish all unions from organizing in the country, and anyone found doing so would be exiled to another country with no way of returning to this country.

The education system would be rewarded for the quality of students they turn out, not for just showing up for the check. Students would be tested for any learning disabilities that would prevent them from learning a certain way and would be given other alternatives to learn. They would be kept in those learning environments until their disability is cured or are ready to support themselves.

There would be no programs that apply only to special groups of Americans. All citizens will have an equal opportunity to learn and succeed in their desired occupation. We want every American to have every opportunity available to them for their success. It's a waste to see talented people not have the chance to fully use their talent in their work.

There would be no life appointments for anyone in any office or position in this country. Everyone who has a position or appointment will keep it on their ability to perform the task required by that position or appointment. Also, there would be a time limit placed on each appointment or position. I realize some positions would require a person to be in that position longer than in other positions.

The census would be electronically taken every five years. People would go to an office and input their information there. The voting would be by city, county, and state, not by voting precincts.

The country's finances would be kept by an independent accounting group, and they would give financial reports to the citizens every four years. The budget would be balanced, and those who violate the trust of the citizens would forfeit their positions and properties to make up for their unauthorized spending. What use is a budget if no one sticks to it?

I would change the currency of the country and reissue new currency when the old is turned in. Every currency coming in from other governments would be examined, and if found to be drug money, it would be kept and burned, not reimbursed. If a foreign country cannot prove that the money was made by legal means, it would be held until that country does prove it. There would be no more Federal Reserve, but an in-house regulatory board would be set up to fill that position, and the three branches of government would each appoint such a board for a five-year term with alternating times for each member.

If any state is found to put its citizens into unreasonable debt, the Federal Government would send an independent auditing group to that state to determine the cause of debt. If determined that it was negligence, those responsible would be obligated to pay back the amount they spent to the state. They would be given a court hearing, and the outcome of that hearing by the state would be enforced by that state.

I would disband the IRS and impose a flat tax that would be collected each month. I would eliminate all state sales tax. Each state has natural resources that belong to the citizens of that state and would be treated as their money if those resources are developed. Any environmental issues would be handled by the state they exist in.

No one in any state or federal government office would be allowed to belong to any world organization As long as they are an elected official of this country. I would not honor any laws that are enforced by any world organization that is in opposition to our core values. I would withdraw from the United Nations until they become a true representation of the people of the world, not a haven for dictators, monarchs, and factious governments.

All legal groups that are in opposition to our country's Constitution and Bill of Rights would not be allowed to operate in this country. Nor would I allow any group of individuals outside of our country to have an active role in our elections in any way. I would eliminate all foreign aid and would only help those countries that ask for our help and are friendly to us.

Our military would be the best trained and best equipped in the world. Each military contract would be given to our country's companies who show they can produce a product superior to all other products like it in the world. Each contract would have a team of experts to oversee the project from start to finish and would have the authority to make decisions in the quality and costs of each piece of equipment produced. This group of experts would be audited on a quarterly basis to make sure everything is done to ensure the desired outcome in a timely manner.

I would not have a military base anywhere; it is not beneficial to our security. I would equally pay our military the going rate of pay for their counterpart in the civilian sector, no more having our military personnel on food stamps and working more than one job to feed their families. Every person who serves more than four years in our armed forces would be given a four-year college tuition to any college of his or her choice. Families who have a member die for this country while serving in the military would be given $500,000.00 as compensation to help the family start a new life.

I do not believe universal health care is a good thing for our country. One reason is that people will take advantage of it. Everyone should have to pay for their health care if possible. What happens with health care for everyone is that the doctors and nurses are not compensated for their hard work and years of training. The best way to maintain an excellent health care system is to attract the best people for health care.

If a family cannot afford health care, then they should be helped, but everyone would have to prove their need for help with their insurance. I would discontinue Medicare for all newcomers in the system and replace it with insurance coverage people could afford. Every employer would provide health care for their employees and be allowed to have a tax write-off for the cost. Once the employee reaches fifty-five years old, they would be given the option, if he or she can afford it, to purchase his or her own insurance. It would be supplemented in cost by the employer, and if the rates go up, the employee would be responsible for the difference. If the employee could not afford the difference, then the government would help to supplement the difference. If each state provided its own health care, it would be better managed by the people of the state for the people in the state. It would involve fewer people than a nationwide health care system and, therefore, would be more manageable.

As for the judicial system, I would overhaul it from top to bottom. I would eliminate all federal courts and give the courts to the states to manage. There would be a federal review system that would manage the states to make sure everyone's constitutional rights are not violated.

I would keep the Supreme Court, but the appointment of judges would be made by Congress and not the president. The Supreme Court judges would serve for only ten years and would be replaced.

The District Court of Appeals would be eliminated, and each state would have their own Court of Appeals. The court system would only be managed by the Federal Government to make sure it is justly administered by each state. Cases that deserve a hearing by the Supreme Court would be heard on a priority basis. I would increase the number of Supreme Court judges to help process the caseload, increasing the number of judges to seventeen instead of nine.

In the appointment process of judges, Congress would only ask pertinent questions. There would be no personal or political questions. Each Supreme Court judge would have only one day of confirmation hearings before being voted on to be appointed a judge to the Supreme Court, not the circus we have now with weeks of confirmation hearings for one judge.

If I were president, these are some of the things I would do.

When you consider your life and what it has meant up to this point and what the future has in store for you, you ask yourself, "Have I made a difference in this world?" Having been a pastor, I have conducted many funerals and have heard many people say wonderful things about the deceased. This is when you ask yourself, "What will people say about my life when I die?"

I asked the owner of a mortuary I knew if I could come to their mortuary and film my funeral or what I would like played at my funeral. Being creative, I came up with this: I would film myself sitting up in the casket and slowly turning toward the people, saying, "I told you I was sick," and then lay slowly back down in the casket. I thought this would leave a lasting impression on people. What do you think? I'm only joking, of course.

# Chapter 23
# THE FUTURE

We all have an opportunity to start a new future right now. A friend of mine felt good about himself. One night, he asked God to allow him to come to heaven to see what it was like. That night, he found himself being picked up by two large angels and taken into the heavens. As they approached the throne room of God, he noticed that it was so quiet it was deafening.

The closer they came to the throne room, the more nervous he got. He realized he wasn't ready to come before the God of the universe in his present condition. One of the angels asked him if he wanted to wait before going into the throne room. With great relief, he said, "Oh yes." He said that if he went into the throne room, he felt he would be burned alive because he had so many things to make right first. He then found himself back in bed with his wife beating on him to wake up. When he awoke, she told him that he was as cold as ice and looked dead. He is a large man and is always hot, so she was afraid he had died. Since this experience, he has tried to clean up his life. Sometimes a good dose of reality can show us that we need a new future and not a repeat of the past.

If I were to change my future, what would I do? I can't change the past, but the past has made me into who I am today. What can make me change the future that is not in my past? I woke up in the middle of the night and found myself standing before the judgment seat of God.

God said, "Bobby, what is in your suitcase?"

I looked, and there beside me was my suitcase. I replied, "You know it's my stuff." God said, "What stuff?"

"It's everything people have done to me and some of what I have done to them."

God looked at me, smiling, and said, "You know, Bobby, we don't let people in here with their suitcases. Go back, and when you have emptied your suitcase and thrown the suitcase away, then come back."

Ever since then, I have been changing my future by having forgiveness today and forgetting the past. Once in a while, I start looking for the suitcase and am reminded of this conversation with God. I have a list of people I have prayed for every day for over forty years. Once in a while, I will have an issue with someone on the list and decide to take him or her off the list. As soon as I think about it, I hear a familiar voice say, "Whose prayer list is this, yours or mine?" Right then, I realize that it is not my list, and I can't take anyone off.

The longer I live, the more God shows me, the more I'm responsible for those things, and I am driven to share these truths with others because of His love for me when I was unlovable. My future is to share all that God has given me to help others. I don't get to choose those He wants me to help. He makes the choice out of His lovingkindness.

Everyone has a right to choose their future, no matter their past. I knew I needed a new life as the one I had was headed for destruction. There was nothing in my future but pain and suffering. I was a large diesel truck running down a narrow mountain road with no breaks and a full load when I was given six words from a man I didn't know, "You can have a new life."

Some people think their lives have been less than exciting. They have obeyed all the rules and have been nice people. They think life has given them a pass on fun. I can't tell you the many times I wish my life had been different for the first twenty-six years. I wasted those vital years on self-centeredness and self-indulgence, not to mention the lives of others I helped destroy. Believe me, living a good life isn't everything, but it sure beats a life of selfishness.

Everyone is doomed to destruction, no matter who they are or what they have or haven't done. It's only by the grace and lovingkindness of God that we have a chance to be saved from our own destruction. Without God's intervention in all of our lives, we would be fodder for this world to use up and then discard us like trash, to be burned on the heap of garbage it perceives us to be. When we take God out of our future, you take away our future.

I had this reoccurring nightmare from as far back as I can remember. Every night, the closet door would open, and pirates would come out and try to drag me into the dark hole they came out of. I would fight them with swords and pistols until I was right at the edge of the dark hole.

Another nightmare was that I was running like the wind, and behind me was a large crocodile with its mouth wide open. I knew that if I stumbled, it would devour me. I spent all my nights fighting to have a future, but in my life, I gave up fighting and was running toward these images of destruction instead of away from them.

This world offers us only those temporal things. It offers us nothing permanent for the future. I'm not storing up things here on earth where someday it will pass away. I'm storing up things in the eternal future where they will remain forever.

Wouldn't you like to go to sleep at night knowing that your future was dependent upon God, who loves you so much that He gave his only Son's life for you so you could have a future without end, a future where you would be valued and loved for eternity? Let's see, I'm trading one death, Jesus's death, for two lives. You're born into this world with a physical body, and then you are born again in Christ, and your eternal spirit comes to life, which gives you two lives. Then your physical body dies, and this leaves you with your eternal spirit. With this eternal spirit, you get to spend eternity in relationship with the God of all creation, His Son Jesus Christ, and everyone else who has made that decision.

There couldn't be a better deal for us.

## Chapter 24
# ENCOUNTER

I attended the Fire Fall Conference at the Vineyard Church in California in 1998. I happened to be at the church for another reason and kept being asked if I was going into the conference. After I had completed my business with the church, I decided to go in for a short time.

I sat there listening to the speaker, and afterward, he called for anyone who wanted prayer to come forward to receive prayer. One of the pastors I knew asked me to help him pray for people. I would stand behind the person he prayed for, and as they collapsed, I would lay them down on the floor.

We did this until another pastor came up to me and asked me to pray for him, which I did, and then he prayed for me. The next thing I knew, two men were trying to move me off the main floor so people could get ready for the evening service; it was 6:00 p.m., and I had been on the floor since noon. I didn't know I would be there for the evening service, but there I was on the floor in the middle of all the people going around me getting ready for the evening service.

Each time the two men tried to move me I could not get up because my stomach was stuck to the floor. I couldn't get it to release, and every time I tried, a wave of power would go through me, and I felt like I got hit with 120 volts of electricity.

After a while, in a vision, I could see Jesus standing on the horizon waving for me to come with Him. Finally, I saw myself going over the horizon hand in hand with Jesus, and then I was released from the floor. At this point, I decided to go to the rest of the conference.

The following day, I was in the meeting and had gone down front to pray for someone who had asked me to pray for him or her earlier. When I got there, I was knocked down onto the steps of the platform with my head stuck to a step in front of me. When I tried to get up, my head would not move from the stage step. Then power would swell up inside of me to the point where I thought I would blow up.

This went on for an hour, and I honestly thought I would die. Out of desperation, I grabbed someone's ankle who was sitting on the steps above me to have something to help me deal with the incredible power inside of me. Every time the power would increase, the person whose ankle I had hold of would get the same power, and he or she would scream. I thought I better let go of this person's ankle, but I couldn't.

Another person began praying for me, and then to release the extreme power in me, I would blow out air from my mouth, and each time I did that, it sounded like a roar. I know this sounds strange, and believe me, it was a traumatic experience for me and the person I had held. After about an hour, I was finally released and could get up, but I was completely out of strength.

I happened to go into another room where there were about fifty Chinese people who wanted someone to pray for them. They grabbed me, and I spent another hour praying for them. They got the same power I had experienced. I had to get to another appointment and tried to get away, but they kept hold of me. I finally got loose and literally ran out of the building. For three days, this power would build up in me every time I went close to the building where the conference was held. I finally took the rest of the week off to rest and recover.

After writing out my story, I can clearly see where I made bad and good decisions. I have learned some important lessons and have noticed some important lessons I have yet to learn. You would think that after seventy years, one would have to conclude that one had learned enough. I have found that no matter how much you have learned, there is always more to life than what you have experienced.

The one thing that has been the most damaging to me was not so much what happened to me but allowing it to control my decisions in life. The bad things we experience in life can distort our ability to make decisions. This is why we need to take in good thoughts and images and discard the old thoughts and images of our past that are not good. Philippians 4:8 says, "Finally, brethren, whatever is pure, whatever is lovely, whatever is of good repute, dwell on these things."

Sometimes a bad outcome is due to bad income in our lives. If you have made decisions based on fear, anger, bitterness, unforgiveness, and jealousy, then you have made decisions based on faulty premises. Sometimes we are taken captive by our thoughts, which our life circumstances have created. Whether those circumstances were good or bad, it makes no difference. Some of us have been imprisoned in our thoughts and don't realize we are prisoners who need to be set free.

# Chapter 25
# CONCLUSION

This is the last chapter, and I ask myself, how do you close your life that hasn't ended yet? I have been on an emotional roller coaster writing this book and haven't a clue on how to end it, but I guess you realize this isn't the last chapter of my life.

My thoughts have always controlled me as everyone has experienced at some time in their lives. How does a person stand back, look at his or her life, and say, "I'm no longer going to let my thoughts control my life"?

How does a person who has had twenty-six years of thoughts controlling him get freed from them? Some people try counseling with a trained counselor, and sometimes that works, and sometimes it doesn't work. Some people try religion, and sometimes it works, and sometimes it doesn't work. Some people give up and end it all by taking their own lives. These are man's attempts to change their lives. My experience is that these things work for a time but only to a lesser degree than desired.

The Aboriginal people believe that each person's life has a story to it, and everything in the story has a song to be sung. I have written a song that is the song of my life, and this book is the story of my life. I'm sharing the words to my song that will come out on Hill Top Record's new album called *America*.

My song is called "All Alone".

Sitting on a curb next to the street,
Darkness surrounding on every side,
Wind blowing and distorting my sight,
Shadows making images in the night.

All looks cold and sounds bring fright,
No one there to comfort and protect,
Imagination out of control,
Bringing images shadows to suspect.

What is in danger is my soul,
All fears take on these terrors,
My peace these shadows have stolen,
Bringing back terrors of past.

How long must I wait to be taken,
Into my house safe at last,
Street is empty all forsaken,
Time is lost in the past.

Unprotected ready to be taken,
Images in the night and fright.

I now have a new story and song. This song is a much happier song, and this life is a much better life. We could all use a happier song and better life. I challenge you to cry out and keep crying out until you receive an answer. There is Someone listening for the cry of your heart, and He has the answer you have always wanted to hear.

"Welcome into the kingdom of God. Now let's get to know each other. I have a new life and song for you."

Love,
Bobby

CPSIA information can be obtained
at www.ICGtesting.com
Printed in the USA
JSHW062137300622
27506JS00001B/3